A TIME TO TRUST

CANDICE GIBBONS

Trilogy Christian Publishers
A Wholly Owned Subsidary of Trinity Broadcasting Network
2442 Michelle Drive
Tustin, CA 92780

Cover design by: Cornerstone Creative Solutions

For information, address Trilogy Christian Publishing
Rights Department, 2442 Michelle Drive, Tustin, Ca 92780.
Trilogy Christian Publishing/ TBN and colophon are trademarks of Trinity Broadcasting Network.

For information about special discounts for bulk purchases, please contact Trilogy Christian Publishing.

Manufactured in the United States of America

10 9 8 7 6 5 4 3 2 1

Library of Congress Cataloging-in-Publication Data is available.

ISBN 978-1-63769-212-7 (Print Book)
ISBN 978-1-63769-213-4 (ebook)

Dedication

*To any girl who has found it seemingly
impossible to trust God*

*To friends and family who long
to know the vivid details*

Contents

Foreword

"No one ever told me grief felt so much like fear."
—C. S. Lewis

Change is inevitable. Whether it comes through the natural process of growing up or moving away from all you have known, it happens to all of us. Unfortunately, just because everyone experiences change doesn't mean it is easy. There is often significant loss. The life that you once knew is over. It has passed on, leaving behind the road of grief. Like Lewis' quote, grief is scary because it involves the unknown. *What happens when everything changes?*

Transitions can either make or break you. Thankfully, there is good news! If you are a follower of Jesus, you have the assurance that "all things work together for the good of those who love God" (Romans 8:28). What a blessing! Because of this, you can count *all* inevitable changes as a natural and beneficial part of life. There is no reason to fear. God has you in His hands. You can thrive through change.

During her fifteen-year-old summer, Candice knew change was coming. Something was happening in our family. Although she couldn't control what we would decide as parents, she did have the choice to trust God or not. Amidst unforeseen sicknesses, relational conflicts, and her deep struggle with trusting in God, her journey forced her to make major choices. Candice, who was at a critical time in her life, chose wisely. Not only did she make the right mental and emotional choices, she acted upon them as well. As her mother, I am deeply proud of her growth and maturity over the past couple of years. She worked hard to rise above what could have easily pulled her down.

My hope is that through her story, you are encouraged and strengthened to face whatever hardships are thrown your way. The reason Candice wrote this book is to follow the scripture that advises us to "encourage one another and build each other up" (1 Thessalonians 5:11). You can learn from her story and apply it to your own situation. Living for God is one big adventure, and it will *always* turn out for good as you follow Him. Candice's story speaks to all of us as we navigate trusting in God even when it doesn't make sense. I pray you are touched by this book and that God speaks to you. No matter the season, no matter the loss, whether you are a young girl becoming a young woman or a young woman becoming an older woman, this story is for you.

With love,
Casey Gibbons
Candice's Mom

"But blessed are those who trust in the Lord and have made the Lord their hope and confidence."

—Jeremiah 17:7

"What Could Happen?"

Six children and a dog race across the green pasture in pure childhood bliss. Shrieks of laughter echo from their mouths, ranging from the young boy's high-pitched squeals to the older girl's motherly cautions.

"Race you to the pond!" strong-willed Bria exclaims, her mane of golden blond hair blowing in the wind.

"Hey! No head starts—" Allison, the preteen sister with black-rimmed glasses and ballet posture, retorts.

"I don't think we should race at all," says Kelly Grace, the second oldest with soft features and silky, caramel blond hair. She is the Beth of the family, the nurturer among her four sisters and little brother. "Let's walk to the pond together," she suggests, loving all things fair.

Angel, the youngest sister with straight, dark chestnut hair and an innocent heart-shaped face, grabs hold of Kelly's hand and turns up her nose at Bria and Allison. "Yeah, *together*," she emphasizes. Everyone knows she is doted on—the family "angel"—and yet no one does anything about it.

"How 'bout it, Candice?" Kelly turns to me, and as the oldest of the family, my vote is the deciding factor. I search Bria and Allison's faces, begging to race, and then see Kelly's warning eyes, motioning her head to little Angel and Jordan.

"Let's run together," I say firmly, throwing Jordan on my back and running towards the pond. I'd like to call myself the Meg of the family; grown-up, well-dressed—the proper sort of peacemaker. But

I am more of a kid at heart, with my denim overalls, bare feet, and freckles; still insisting on my own way in life even if it's wrong—like the time I was two and sat in protest at the counter for an entire afternoon because my mom told me to eat a popsicle. Mom had to replace the popsicle three times so it would last through during my rebellion. Why in the world I didn't just enjoy the treat and move on to climb a tree, I'll never know…but suppose little Candice just didn't feel like eating a popsicle that day. Anyways, little Candice didn't eat the popsicle after all. Because whatever she wants happens.

Erase the image of a little pigtailed farm girl gallivanting in the field. I am five feet nine inches and a half, constantly battling to uphold straight posture, and my feet naturally curve in like a newborn baby deer. I am not a farmer's daughter, but I'll take the outdoorsy title since I do proudly bring my hiking stick into the town post office when I get the mail. I don't really mind being an awkward sort of girl, skipping down grocery aisles and whistling movie soundtracks and practicing my British accent at drive-thru windows. But I'm most certainly *not* your ordinary teenager. I am Candice Gibbons, and Candice doesn't do anything normal or easy or—worst of all—*average*.

So, here I am, living life as an ordinary Midwest teenager, pausing just before I reach the pond to wisp the wild brown hairs out of my eyes to gaze back at our yellow childhood cottage. There are usually cows in this pasture, but Mr. Coggins, our neighboring farmer who lets us run in his field, has them grazing somewhere else today. My good ol' dog Charlie beats us to the waterfront, barking loudly at the fish in the water.

"Summer's here!" Bria drops down onto a dry spot of grass.

"I love summer!" Angel smiles.

"Time for swimming," Bria splashes a bit of pond water on Allison's face.

"Time for reading," Kelly reflects.

"*Bria!*" Allison wipes her glasses and scowls.

"…and time for cotton candy!" toddler-aged Jordan, the youngest in the family, adds out of the blue.

"*Cotton candy?*" Kelly asks.

"I think summer is the time for ice cream," says Allison, always dreaming about some sort of treat.

"Time for *freedom*," I mutter, laying on a pile of straw and studying the clouds. Now that my freshman year of high school has finally come to an end, I am ready for my own adventure. Something new. Something exciting!

Ding! Ding! Ding!

"*Time for supper!*" Mom's faint voice mixes with the ringing of porch chimes as she calls us to eat, "*Hot cheeseburgers and watermelon waiting!*"

"Now, *this* is summer," Bria dashes to her feet and follows the smoke from Dad's grill.

While the children run ahead, I pause and soak in a panoramic view of country paradise.

I live in the magical land of Ozark, Missouri. You wish you lived here, but only a few of us are fortunate enough to call it home. It's as if the sun is constantly shining, the birds are always singing, and even the trash can guy whistles while he works. Okay, I've never actually *heard* him whistle, but I bet he would because he's lucky to work in the land of Oz. Imagine soft breezes, wind chimes, thick green grass, colorful flower beds, deep green oak trees, American flags waving on every wraparound porch, and picturesque sunrises and sunsets— that's Ozark. And when you live among twenty-ish cousins and a mixture of uncles, aunts, and grandparents, your whole life revolves around some kind of celebration.

My mom's parents, Papa and Annie, are the Alabama-accented, *Roll-Tide* fans full of love and laughter. Whether it's the 1940s romance album ringing through the house on repeat, the gentle sway of Annie's porch bed swing, or playing a friendly round of Chinese checkers with Papa, a night at their house is one of great fellowship.

Annie is adventurous and exciting, ready to support your ideas and actually make them happen. "Cruisin' Tuesdays" is just one of the traditions she started to host a weekly night of highway riding, soda drinking, sixties-music-singing fun to enjoy Missouri's summer nights. Papa is the photographer of the family, capturing each grand-child's life in a personal way. He is wise and compassionate, always reading some sort of book and sharing his insights about the deep matters of life.

My dad's family members are also southern: a Mississippi-bred crowd that gathers at my grandparents' farm called Riverview Ranch. My grandma, Gigi, is known for her distinguished southern cooking and sophisticated charm, generously welcoming us with a kiss on the cheek and a kitchen towel in hand. My grandpa, Poppy, is a dreamer—continuously planning some sort of fun. He loves movies like me, and through the years, he's hired three different film companies to create our own family western movies—the last one was even premiered in our local theater. Look up the definition of big dreams—it's Poppy.

Weekends at the farm are spent fishing, hunting, riding horses, picking off cherry tomatoes from Poppy's Garden, screaming at the TV during an *Ole Miss* football game, cooking with Gigi in her famous kitchen, and grilling the game my uncles catch in the woods. Overall, both sides of my family are wildly expressive, intimately southern, and full of generous hospitality.

The farm roads connecting Ozark rest on stomach-turning, corner-weaving hills, fondly called the "Ozark Mountains." Those roads lead to my childhood church, school, friends' houses, Annie and Papa's house, Riverview Ranch, and one good Walmart. There is a sense of simplicity and familiarity breathed into the small-town shops, family-run diners, and Farmer's Market freshness. But most importantly, Missouri is home. Always has been, always will be.

"You're *what*?" my friend Sophia gasps incredulously, sitting up from her sun-tanning position by the edge of the pool.

"You heard me; I have to travel twelve hours in the car to visit my mom's relatives in Alabama for a week," I repeat, rolling my eyes underneath my sunglasses.

Here's to my time for freedom. Now I am going to miss a week of summer to visit my great Aunt Wendy and great-grandfather, Grandaddy.

"Picture this, Sophia: me, squished beside six other people in a car packed with stuffed animals and blankets for *twelve hours*." I kick my feet in the water and stare at the sky.

I've been swimming at Sophia's neighborhood pool for generations of summers. We've known each other since we were three. We're both tall (she's two inches taller than me) and have long hair, though hers is naturally blond. Sophia is an energetic cheerleader who works at the local McDonald's.

"Are you even excited?" she picks up the conversation.

"You're kidding. I've been looking forward to summer freedom for weeks…no, make that since school started!" I rub water on my arms.

Sophia pats my back. "You poor, spoiled Missouri girl. If this is as hard as your life gets…"

"Hey, I know I don't have a job or car like you, but I've got my own problems," I defend playfully. The sun is beginning to scorch down on us, and I'm tempted to put on another layer of sunscreen.

"I don't know what you mean by *summer freedom*, but at least you'll only be gone a week," she emphasizes like I have an error in my logic. "Didn't you say you wanted something to change?"

"Not change, just excitement," I clarify. "There's a difference."

"You sound flexible," she says dryly.

"I know, I know," I acknowledge. "I need to be less stubborn. But I'm not as bad as I was when I was three, right?"

Sophia laughs and avoids the question. "We better get back to the house," she stands and stretches her arms. "*That's* going to hurt tonight," she stares at my legs. Sure enough, they're as red as Poppy's cherry tomatoes.

"At least I'll have a good tan by the time I get to Alabama…"

"Oh yeah, your great-grandpa will sure appreciate your nice tan," Sophia says sarcastically. I elbow her. With a real job and a cool car, she's like my older sister. And here I am, a fifteen-year-old freshman who still rides with her mom, complaining about one week of the year. I need to grow up, but not today. Not yet.

"Wanna race up the hill?" I ask.

"Beat you there!"

So much for planning my own summer. I grumble on my bed, staring up at the ceiling. I've had to decline *three* pool party invitations, all because of this vacation to Alabama. As soon as I get back from the trip, it will be time to pack my bags for a writing competition I attend every year, and soon after, I'll be on the bus headed to youth camp.

"Please get out!" Kelly bursts into the room, juggling her array of pink-colored clothes in a pile of laundry.

"Why?"

"Grace is about to call me, and I want privacy." She drops her laundry on the pink polka-dotted twin bed across from me. I hop off my squeaky twin and race down the stairs with no specific destination. Good grief, a fifteen-year-old needs her space. Hasn't it been enough that we've shared a room for the majority of my life?

You're so selfish, a thought pops in my mind. On this unflattering thought, I run downstairs in pursuit of fresh air. Nature seems to calm me down. I slide open the glass door that leads to the back porch, head to the dusty brown porch swing and fling myself on its cushions. The breeze is warm and gentle. Mom's hanging chimes ding in their usual manner, reminding me of the simplicity of my childhood. Not that it's ended, I just feel like things are changing. Like how this trip to Alabama came out of absolutely nowhere and is disrupting my plans. I don't like change, though, so I'm not going to focus on it.

I lean back on the swaying swing and hang my feet in the air, staring at the four acres of green pasture. Besides the ringing chimes, there isn't a sound for miles. Pure, country stillness. There's an old oak tree at the edge of the yard, the scenic cow pasture behind it. The

Great Oak and I have become lifelong companions. It is the tallest among all of the trees in the yard. I'm guessing it's going on fifty years or so of living. He's a faithful one.

Should I feel guilty for making such a fuss over sharing a room? I mean, most of my friends have the same problem, and I guess they've accepted it. But once my mind is set on something, it is nearly impossible to relent. Though I *wish* I weren't so stubbornly selfish.

"What do you think?" I pitch to Mom tonight as she finishes the dishes.

"You'll have to ask Dad when he gets home from Chicago," she wipes her stray blond hairs with her forearm and dries her hands. In moments like this, it makes me wish Dad didn't travel so much. This is the last time I am going to campaign for my own room, and I am desperate for an answer. Thankfully, Mom senses my urgency and lets me ask Dad on the phone.

He says yes!

I can't believe it—my speech actually worked! It's not as if I doubted all too much that it wouldn't; I just never assumed my problems would disappear this fast. I do have a good track record, though. When I was twelve, I won the debate over whether I could get a dog, and—boom—it worked again! I know this means preteens Bria and Allison will have to share a room, but it's not like I haven't paid my time. And get this—Mom even said I could shop for some basic décor! I'm planning on calling Sophia over to help decorate once we get back from Alabama. By then, I should have all of my ideas pinned down.

Now that I feel such joy and invincibility, it reminds me of how conditional I am, relying on outward circumstances to dictate my attitude. But forget deep thoughts—it's time to enjoy summer.

"I vote Sonic."

"No, Braum's ice cream is the best!"

"But I want McDonald's."

"Fine." Annie's head swivels as she slams the breaks. She raises her hands off the wheel in submission and then addresses the opinions in the back seat. "Bria, you pick where we're going to eat our main meal," she points. "Allison, choose a place where we'll get a side. Angel, you can pick somewhere to pick up dessert. Kelly, we'll go wherever you want for our drink. "Oh, and Candice," she turns to me in the passenger seat. "Be our DJ tonight."

"Hooray!" shouts consent to the proposal. And so, we are off: me, in the front seat pressing play on the Beach Boys CD in the old car console, and my four sisters dancing in the back seat with their hair blowing in the wind from the late-night Missouri breeze.

Tonight is a girls-only Cruisin' Tuesday.

Annie has a way of making ordinary events unforgettable, like the time she packed us in Mom's old blue minivan and said we were going to Kentucky. Excited and confused, no one knew what to think until we arrived at the Kentucky Fried Chicken restaurant and were ordered to hop out and take a picture. That's how Annie rolls.

"Summer is the best!" I grin, dangling my arm out the window. We speed down the highway, singing at the top of our lungs.

"Are you coming to my house this weekend?" she leans over to me.

"Of course I am!" I yell above the wind. "I wouldn't miss a Sunday." Quite literally, I don't know the last time I did miss a weekend at the farm or a Sunday at Annie's house. That's my absolute favorite part of summer—spending time with my grandparents.

Annie pats my shoulder. "You're one blessed kiddo," she tells me.

"I know." I smile back.

For a split second, I forget about the trip to Alabama. I feel so carefree and confident. Come to think of it, I've felt this way my entire life…maybe I've taken this freedom for granted.

"No, no, no. That picture was taken at the Bricks' Valentine's Dinner two years ago. See—my hair is twice as long." Ella whisks her hair in front of her shoulders to make her point.

"Okay, I get it," Diana acknowledges, scrolling to the next picture of everyone standing in front of a restaurant.

"Hey! You know where we should go for next year's Bricks' Valentine's Dinner? That new fancy Mexican restaurant downtown!" Catherine suggests, her intelligence inspiring new ideas.

"Ooh, yes!" I squeal. Now everyone's chiming in, interrupting each other by the who-has-the-loudest-voice method. It's a fight to the finish.

"Bricks, *please* be quiet," Mom calls down the hall. "I know you're having fun because it's summer and, well, you're the Bricks, but Jordan just fell asleep."

Giggling subsides, but only momentarily.

There are twelve of us—all girls—and we met at a homeschool co-op. Mondays are our "in-person" school days where we gather for peer review and teacher assessment at a local church, and then we do school at home the rest of the week. When a bunch of homeschooled girls have spent Mondays together since 7th grade, it's common knowledge that inside jokes make up 99 percent of our conversations. (I bet Juicy Juice doesn't mean anything to you other than drinking grape juice on your grandmother's porch, but it has its own meaning with us. Enough said.)

Each member of our high school sorority—each "Brick"—is unique in style, and we respect that. You can wear whatever you want, talk however you want, and even use your preferred color of pencil. We couldn't care less. We're simply bound together by the values of faith and friendship.

Half of us are dancers, musicians, singers, or public speakers, and the other half are graphic artists, clothing designers, avid academics, or brilliant storytellers. Eighth-grade lunch breaks exposed our creativity; we saw them as opportunities to create short films about anything in sight: chips, straws, talking logic textbooks, and Mrs. Myers' hand soap—or anything *out* of sight—secret alien invasions, black holes, an imaginary man-sized rabbit named Harvey or fossils underground (yes, we crawled under a building for this one). It's no wonder we developed the reputation for being the most...er, *creative* class in the school.

But truthfully, our main bonds are formed standing in a circle, holding hands, and praying over each other during our weekly Bible study with my mom, created so everyone can keep their hearts right with God—*that's* what makes a Brick a Brick.

My close friend, Diana, who's the sensible leader of the Bricks, shuts the computer screen. "I'm spent. Let's finish looking at old pictures tomorrow."

"Good idea," Kelly agrees.

It's nearly 1 a.m., but who's checking the time? "But...but..." I stutter.

"Tomorrow, Candice." Soft-spoken Grace pats my shoulder as my adventurous friend Catherine and I reluctantly snuggle into our sleeping bags, we can't help but snicker.

"*Harvey,*" she whispers mysteriously, referring to the name of a literature play we studied that inspired our belief in the invisible rabbit. All it takes is the whispered word *"Harvey"* to rouse the room.

"*Harvey! Harvey! Harvey!*" the room chants. I zip open my sleeping bag and sit on my knees, pumping my fist in the air.

"Oh look, is that Harvey's shadow over there in the window?" Lexi gasps, pointing outside.

"*It is!*" I shriek.

"*Ahh!*" Everyone jumps up and runs around the room, all except Diana, who simply smiles and shakes her head. We're seconds away from Mom flinging open her bedroom door in her gray, flowery housecoat to silence us for good, but I can't control myself. Now that we've survived our freshmen year of high school, it's time to party!

"See you in two weeks!" I wave to the Bricks. Like all sleepovers, morning arrived all too quickly. I'm tired, but it's that good kind of tiredness you get from sleepovers where you sacrifice sleep for friendship bonding. Charlie scampers up to me.

"You want to go on a walk, boy?"

He wags his tail and spins in a circle.

"Candice," Mom calls from the kitchen, "would you mind setting out lunch for the family?"

Ugh. I clench my teeth. *I would rather not, thank you,* I mutter, but then I feel convicted. "Can Charlie and I go on a walk?" I yell back, hoping I don't sound frustrated.

"That's fine, go ahead. I'm already in here, anyway," she mutters, slightly frustrated. "Don't forget to help pack Angel's suitcase for Alabama!"

Close one. I run through the house and grab Charlie's leash from the cabinet in the laundry room, which is stuffed with suitcases. That reminds me I should probably be packing for that dreaded trip to Alabama. But who am I to complain? With my own room on its way, this summer is already looking much brighter than usual. What could go wrong?

"There's a Prophecy"

Hot. The one word I see, feel, and breathe is hot.

Who knew the Alabama humidity would fry my tediously curled hair? I feel like a total frizz ball walking into Grandaddy's church service, and I can tell by the looks of others that it's actually that bad. Thankfully, Mom gives me a hair tie to throw my used-to-be-curled hair into a bun. *So much for a Sunday style.*

Oh, great. By the looks of Aunt Wendy, I can tell my dress is way too short for this kind of church service. I keep hearing the *tsk-tsk* sound she makes to her husband, Uncle John. But what's a girl supposed to do when it feels like 130 degrees?

"I'm surprised your daddy let you out of the house like that," she says in the church lobby, looking me up and down. Thankfully, Mom is in the restroom with Angel and Jordan, or else she would have sided with her aunt. I bet my dress wasn't even *designed* to be short, but one of the downfalls of being tall is how everything automatically looks too short or too tight. *Oh, if only I were short...*

Though these Alabama southern accents sound like everyone who lives here is related to me, everything else feels uncomfortable and unfamiliar. So far, the trip has been nothing more than trekking to tourist attractions in the heat of a furnace, being introduced to relatives I've never met, and eating casseroles. But the church service itself isn't too bad.

As worship comes to a close and everyone is seated on the formal pews, I feel a rush of wind circulate the chapel. *So, this church has an air conditioner unit, after all.* I smile, closing my eyes and breathing it in while it lasts. The room is still hot and musty, and I gather my siblings feel the same way. Grandaddy, who was a proud colonel in the National Guard, sits as straight as a board beside Uncle John, my fun-loving cousin Maggie, and Aunt Wendy, who is sitting by Mom, who holds Jordan in her lap. My sisters are beginning to sweat as I am, and I wonder just how long this service is supposed to last.

Don't get me wrong; I love church. It's the world I was born into. My dad has served in ministry for over twenty-five years, and that makes me an automatic "PK" (Pastor's Kid). My entire life has revolved around the church world, and it's something I see as a blessing. I'm a good Christian PK, but I wouldn't call myself one of those die-hard believers. I've watched my parents live out what it means to live like Jesus: to love others unconditionally, to live righteously, and to walk by faith. And they're genuinely happy in life, which is what we all want to experience, right? If God works for them, maybe He'll work for me.

Still, church or no church, new atmospheres like this make me feel uncomfortable. I have this longing to go home, back to familiarity. I miss the comfortable church chairs back in Missouri. Dad's preaching in Chicago this weekend, so he didn't come with us on the trip, and when he's away, I feel this twinge of vulnerability, something I've felt since I was about five. It started when I was on a trip with my grandparents, and I missed Dad, but I couldn't talk to him because he was preaching. When this feeling comes, my heart starts to race, my mouth gets hot, and I feel like I'm going to cry.

I can't sit still. I feel inferior in this dress, my frizzy hair is driving me crazy, and I don't like being away from Dad. I know I need to get over myself, but it's easier said than done. Besides, how's a girl supposed to overcome her feelings so quickly? I should focus on something else...*anything* besides what's going on in front of me. I want to go home. Design my new room. Play with Charlie. I'd do anything but sit through this hour-long service to go back to Missouri.

As I begin to brainstorm design ideas for my room and then agitate myself over being on this bothersome trip, the pastor's words catch my attention.

"I believe God is about to prompt someone in here to step out and make a difference for His kingdom," he prophesies in a southern drawl.

This is nothing new. When you've been a pastor's kid your whole life, it's as if there is no such thing as a new sermon. *Just ignore it and get back to your drawing*, I tell myself.

"God is calling some of you to step out of your comfort zones into a great adventure, and your obedience and sacrifice will lead to great blessings." Once again, his words interrupt my thoughts.

Well, God. I've been at church since the day I was born. We're good friends, right?

Silence.

If you really want to bless your faithful Christian Candice down here on planet earth, I'd love to win that writing competition coming up, I say in my head.

I have something bigger for you, a voice whispers.

I've never felt as if God was talking directly *to* me, but if I were to guess what it would feel like, this would be it. *But what could God possibly want to do with me?*

Do you trust me? It's like God is flat-out asking me.

Of course, I trust you, I answer back, *you're God!*

My mind begins to race. My heart starts pounding like a drum. *What if God is about to call me to do something radical—like be a missionary to Africa or become the first kid millionaire? No, scratch that last one. Too selfish.* Excitement overwhelms me, though I don't know why. This sort of thing has never happened to me before. It's like this inner joy is springing up within my heart, and I can't stop it.

God would use me?! I smile to myself. Ever since I was little, I always pictured myself as a world changer…whatever that meant. Mom and Dad still tell me, "You are a leader" and "You can change the world," but it's different now. I mean, what kid *didn't* think they were unstoppable? I'm fifteen, for crying out loud. I just hope I can survive geometry.

It's time for you to make a difference. It's as if God is answering my own question.

The thought of little ol' Candice, elevated in the world, making a radical impact like directing an Oscar-winning film or solving world hunger makes me grin and even chuckle a bit.

The unthinkable is happening.

"He's talking about your family!" Aunt Wendy whispers down the pew.

Wait a minute…Aunt Wendy is in on this too? Is this all some kind of setup?

Maybe my Alabama relatives conspired with the pastor to preach some message to scare me…

Probably not. I dismiss the thought when Kelly looks at me with wide eyes filled with excitement.

"I feel it, too," she whispers in my ear. *Oh, my goodness!*

Now I know I'm not the only one who senses something supernatural, and it's freaking me out. We're not supposed to talk in church, and definitely not in a church like this one. The fact that Aunt Wendy, a born-again Bible believer spoke up, means it's serious. Thank goodness Grandaddy can't hear her, or he'd have a fit.

But why did she say our *family*?

As we continue to listen to the pastor's message, I am growing increasingly uncomfortable. Words like "obedience" and "sacrifice" echo from the microphone. I glance down the row and see Mom silently crying, muttering words about how our family is being "summoned by God." *Aw man, I thought this special calling was exclusively for me.*

"…And God will give you blessings on the other side of your obedience." The pastor closes his message with a solemn grin. *That's it? No specific clues or directions?*

As the church members clear out of the sanctuary, our row remains still. I search everyone's faces and find that they feel the same feeling that I do. Even Jordan is quietly sitting in Kelly's lap. *Does anyone know what's going on here?*

"I feel it in my bones," Aunt Wendy tells Mom as they continue to talk about the service.

While the kids swim in Aunt Wendy's pool, Mom and I pack in Aunt Wendy's red convertible sports car to pick up some fried chicken. I squeeze in the tiny back seat and seriously pray we don't crash.

"What on earth do you mean?" Mom asks, holding onto the car handle as we swerve out of the driveway.

"You know I have the gift of prophecy." Aunt Wendy taps her head of silver hair and takes her eyes off the road to look at me.

"Careful Aunt—"

"God is doin' something in y'all's family; I just know it," she interrupts Mom's instructions, swerving back in her lane. I do feel pretty cool in the back seat of her Camaro, even though there is no seatbelt and zero legroom. I stare out the window and hum the soundtrack from the movie *Up*, trying to block out the sour words of "moving" and "change."

Why am I stressing about this? It's nothing more than Aunt Wendy trying to get us to be missionaries or something. I'm blowing this whole ordeal out of proportion. Surely it's just a cool sermon thought. Why should I be worried?

Maybe it's because I'm pretty confident in my world right now. A little too comfortable. That's why this whole *"Change is coming"* propaganda is getting on my nerves. In fact, this whole trip is driving me crazy. I just want to go home.

After we order the chicken, or rather, Aunt Wendy orders her pick for us, we fill our cups with sodas and sit in a sticky red booth and discuss the pastor's words.

"Do you think we're going to adopt children?" Mom asks, a glimmer of hope in her eyes.

We were a foster family for twelve kids at different points in life, and ever since Mom's been unable to have more children, her heart is set on adopting. But if you ask me, there are already too many kids.

I leave the table to collect some straws and napkins. If only I could've stayed home, I could be with Sophia at the pool right now. And I'm all for serving God, but God should know by now that I'm rooted in Missouri…as in, I can't imagine my life anywhere else. If Missouri were to have a billboard promoting the most devoted teenage Missourian, my face would be on it.

Is this really God speaking? I debate in my head, waiting for a chance to grab the straws. *Because if it isn't God, there's nothing to worry about.* I nod my head at my logical thought. This guy in front of me is taking forever, meticulously emptying the ketchup machine with dozens of little paper cups.

If it IS God, would I deliberately disobey Him? The thought hits me out of nowhere.

I freeze. The ketchup guy has finally moved out of the way, but my feet feel like they're in heavy cement blocks instead of shoes. My hands are shaking as I fumble for a pile of straws. All I can picture is the illustrations in my childhood Bible about Jonah and the Whale, where Jonah is swallowed by a giant fish because he ran from God. My eyes widen. *Would I be swallowed by a giant fish if I didn't obey?*

"No," Aunt Wendy's voice yells from the table, whisking me back to reality.

"We're not adopting?" I hear Mom ask as I approach the table.

"Do you think Dad's back is going to be healed from pain?" I light up. Dad ruptured a disk and hurt other areas of his back while playing college football, and he lives in excruciating pain. I've learned how to massage him and relieve some pain, though I know it is not enough. I have been praying for healing in my dad's back for as long as I can remember.

"No, sweetheart, it's not about your dad, though we do pray for him," she says slowly, stacking the napkins on the sticky table.

"What about my feet? Do you think they'll be miraculously healed, and I can dance again?" The question comes out before I process what I'm saying. Since eighth grade, I have had screws in both sides of my feet to repair the curve in my bones. The hardest part was having to quit dance—which used to be what I lived for—and dealing with foot pain every day. I can't wear normal shoes or even walk very far without my nerves burning with pain.

"Maybe your feet will be healed, but I feel like it's gonna be something for your family like y'all are going to move somewhere."

Just what I dreaded, I think to myself, slowly sipping my water.

"Where is your dad this weekend, anyway?" Aunt Wendy asks.

"Chicago," Mom says perplexed, "you don't think we're moving there, do you?"

"I don't know, Casey, but my gut tells me you are."

I nearly choke at her words.

"Aunt Wendy, there's no way!" Mom exclaims.

"Aunt Wendy, that would be the same as us moving to the moon," I retort. Aunt Wendy is a missionary to India, so maybe to her, moving isn't that big of a deal. But if God is calling us on some wild goose chase like moving to Chicago, we really might as well paint our faces, shave our heads and run around in our swimsuits.

In short, there's absolutely *no way* I am going to let this happen.

"Impossible!"

"Coming through!" One of my uncles reaches his burly, hairy arm across Gigi's bowl of fruit salad to grab a smoked rib. I am sitting next to my good cousin Ryan, who's fourteen, at the kids' table. *Someday I'll be old enough to move to the adult table*, I think to myself, looking down at all of the cousins squished at the folding table draped with a red tablecloth.

It's the Fourth of July weekend, and this is one of those seldom precious times that Dad is home. He travels often between states like Texas, Oklahoma, and Illinois. I can already predict the schedule of tonight: eat a filling supper, make homemade peach ice cream, play a game of wiffleball with the cousins and end the night with fireworks in the field. I love holidays at the farm, and though I can predict the actions of each of our dramatic family members, I never grow tired of them.

I've had a lot to think about since our trip to Alabama. What began as a pointless week of misery was one of the most interesting encounters I've ever had—and that's serious for a church kid to say. Aunt Wendy's words still ring in my ears: *"God is doin' something in y'all's family."* Like what? Surely, it's not a move. In Missouri, I'm grounded. Established. Single and loving it. Whatever those clichés are about small-town girls, it's me. Besides, I can't imagine a weekend away from the farm. It's the event center of our family get-togethers, the central hub of entertainment. I imagine we would practically feel disowned if we left.

Thank goodness I'm a master at distracting myself from hard questions. I bite into a hot, homemade roll drenched with butter and decide to think about Youth Camp. After all, it is just one week away. I'm counting the days to see my sisterly friend Jaclyn from church and have a week of teenage fun. Camp has always been a place I can slip away and process life, which is something I desperately need right now.

I need to search for an opportunity to hear Dad's read on the prophecy we heard in Alabama, but it seems like every family member is vying for his attention. I glance over at the adult table and notice Angel and Jordan sitting in his lap and pulling at his shirt. Dad's brothers, who are well over six feet and decked out in camo and sports gear, are reenacting one deer hunting story after another. I hear the chime of my aunts' laughter in the kitchen, busily preparing the puddings, pies, and other desserts.

Despite my vain attempts, I'm having a hard time enjoying myself. I mean, what am I supposed to feel when God is stirring our hearts about change in the family?

Look at Mom, I think to myself. I watch her flip her long, blond hair into a thick ponytail and tie an apron around her waist. *She seems so happy. Doesn't she remember the church service in Alabama? Isn't she worried that something is going to happen?*

Obviously, she's not. Or maybe she's hiding it and putting it on a front.

After supper, I pull away into the dimly lit family room and find Dad alone, stretching his back on the couch.

"Hi, Candy Cane," he calls me by my childhood nickname, reaching out for a hug.

"Can we talk for a minute?" I ask, offering to rub his shoulders.

"Of course, we can," he says.

"I've been meaning to talk to you about something that happened in Alabama." I'm not sure what to say next. My heart is beating out of my chest. I can't tell if I'm more nervous or excited. *But why would I be excited?* "I felt like God was speaking to me—to us—at the Sunday service."

Dad smiles, "God is always speaking to us."

"No, I mean…er, like I actually heard his voice." I scrunch up my face, searching for the right words.

"Oh?"

"Yeah. I know it may sound weird, but I took a lot of good notes…" I fumble around for the church notecard I tucked inside my phone case after the trip. "Here." I hand him the card. To my embarrassment, it's flipped to the side where I drew the sketches of my dream room.

"Not that side," I turn it awkwardly to the back, showing him a jumbled paragraph of verse references and keywords: *Obedience. Sacrifice. Blessings.*

"Aunt Wendy thinks we're moving to Chicago," I say the notion like it's incredulous. If there's anyone who loves Missouri more than I do, it's Dad.

Dad laughs. Steady, level-headed, and in no rush to jump to conclusions, I've always agreed with his logic. Still, because I felt the same eerie feeling Aunt Wendy did, I'm not inclined to completely reject it.

"Is she sure it's Chicago?" his words catch my attention.

I stare back in disbelief. "What are you saying?"

"Well, you know there are other churches who have offered our family pastoring positions, like Minnesota, Oklahoma, Florida…"

"Dad, are you serious?" I slowly inch away. "You don't think we would actually *move*, do you?"

"I hope not. I *pray* not," Dad says solemnly. "The only way I would move would be if God told us directly. But Candy Cane," he strokes my hair, "I do feel like God is doing something unique in our family."

I can hardly believe my ears. *If Dad doesn't think it's outrageous, this might happen!*

I shoot off the couch. "This is crazy. Absolutely crazy!"

"I know. Nothing like this has happened in your life…" he says as if every kid goes through this at a certain age. *Yeah, right.* This is literally a move of God—right here in our family. *What else is going to happen?*

"A tie for 26th place, that's what." I slam the judge's papers on the kitchen counter and let out a huff of frustration. Determined to win first place at the writer's competition I attended, I had been clinging to the hope of winning all week. But now, it's over, and I am home facing the depressing scores.

"Oh, Canzie. It can't be *that* bad," Mom tries to console me by saying her newly created nickname for me. It's too late; I'm boiling with frustration.

"Considering I threw my life into that book chapter and didn't even place the top ten, apparently something's wrong." I cover my face with my hands.

Mom reaches for my manuscript and flips to the summary. "You wrote about a girl who loses her grandmother…"

"Yep," I confess through gritted teeth.

"…but you've never lost your grandmother…"

"Well, yeah," I admit. "But remember when I lost my pet bunny, Leonardo, when I was twelve? I made everyone come to the outdoor funeral and help me bury him. That was a pretty big deal."

"It's not exactly the same thing as losing a loved one."

"Leo was my true love."

"I mean a family member or an unexpected loss like leaving something you love."

I can't argue with that. "I guess I'm not a good writer…"

"I wouldn't say that. You just need to write about something you've personally experienced, something the reader can identify with in their own life."

I lift my head from the table and wipe away the hair in front of my eyes.

"Maybe soon we'll know what it feels like…" I say slowly.

"What do you mean?"

"*Don't you see?*" I throw my hands in the air. "Ever since the trip to Alabama, it's like we're running against the tide. I am trying to enjoy summer, but all I can think about is that weird message about God telling us that change is coming. It's as mysterious as the *winds of change* people talk about. Kind of spooky if you ask me."

"You don't trust God, do you?"

I'm caught off guard by her question.

"I mean, He's brought you this far, hasn't He?" she rubs my back.

"I just don't want to lose our home," I choke out the words.

Mom is quiet. I think I've struck a nerve. I know for a fact she is against the thought of moving or anything related to it. Still, she knows as well as I do that change is coming. It's such a vague warning.

"We won't lose anything unless…unless God has something else better for us," she reasons as if to comfort herself more than anything. "And the way I see it, the chances of us leaving Missouri are next to impossible."

Yeah, right.

Stop overreacting, Candice, I coach myself. *We aren't moving because Dad said he wouldn't move unless God told him directly. And so far, moving is nothing more than a hypothetical concept.*

Since the conversation with Mom, I've thought a lot about moving, but not like it's a serious issue. It's just a change in the air; nothing more, nothing less. Besides, my mind has already switched its attention to the best week of summer: youth camp. I can't wait to detach from all of this confusion and enjoy the great outdoors. Jaclyn and I, born and raised pastor's kids, have gone to camp together since second grade. We don't see each other outside of church and youth camp, but by the time we're sitting on the camp bus again, it's like we never left.

Jaclyn, tall, courageous, and blessed with thick caramel curls, is a natural trendsetter. Her joy is contagious. Her heart is genuine. She reminds me to live in the real world, like the time she convinced me to sign up for a mission trip.

"Come on, you can spare a week to go play with underprivileged children," she told me during spring break, pushing me out of my comfort zone. And before I had time to shoot down her idea, we were on our way to an inner-city kids' center to share Jesus' love. It was one of the best weeks of my life.

Jaclyn is the model PK if there ever was one. Her life literally revolves around church—whether it's helping with kids, playing the guitar on the worship team, or leading a junior high small group. A few weeks ago, after service, she even encouraged me to start a Wednesday night podcast with some student leaders at youth group.

"There's *no way* I could host that."

"But who else will? Your dad is Scotty Gibbons!"

"So?"

"So, you're the amazing pastor's daughter, that's what. You're a natural at bringing impactful stories out of teenagers. Just ask them the right questions, and they'll talk," she encouraged.

It was as if she said, *"Get out of your own head"* through her expression, throwing her arm around me and staring into my eyes.

"You're right," I admitted after a long pause. "But I'm going to interview you first, so come prepared."

"You know I don't like to speak in front of people!" Jaclyn's eyes grew wide.

"Well, that makes two of us." I patted her on the back and stood up. "Hey, we're already friends, so we should sound totally natural together. That is if we don't laugh our way through it!"

Jaclyn laughed. "Fine. I'll do it if you'll go first."

Excitement fills the air as youth leaders load the buses, give us our team wristbands and do the head check for lice. As usual, PK Candice has been here a good hour before all of the other campers, sitting idly in the atrium looking for Jaclyn, who's usually running all over the place.

"There you are!" I hear her familiar voice across the lobby amidst dozens of rowdy teenagers. She's wearing a green T-shirt (that's our team color), and her curls are woven into thick Dutch braids. I wave and call out to her above the noise.

"Did you bring your earbuds?" I ask once she gets closer. Jaclyn smiles mischievously.

"Of course, but you know the rules about electronics. My mom wouldn't let me bring my phone, so we're going to have to use yours." It didn't help our little secret that her mom, the kid's pastor, is a camp counselor, but I'm more likely to take risks than she is, and my conscience says that we'll be okay.

"I'll have you to thank if you get us suspended from camp for the rest of high school," she jokes, elbowing me. Suddenly, my heart stops. *What if this is my last camp with Jaclyn?* The words haunt me as I numbly follow the crowd outside to the buses. *Woah. I've never experienced "last time" circumstances like this…ever.*

Jaclyn is continuing to talk, but I don't hear a word she's saying.

"Isn't that crazy?" her last words snap me out of my trance.

"Huh?"

"You weren't listening." She rolls her eyes, wearing the expression my mom has when I forget to do something.

"Sorry, I'm just excited," I cover up, giving her a hug. *C'mon, Candice. Be happy.*

Be happy? I argue with myself. *Everything's not okay. Face it!*

We continue onto the buses, pull out her earbuds, and snack on a family-sized bag of Sour Patch Kids all the way to the campground.

"I wonder what the new campground in Oklahoma is like," I overhear a junior high girl say in front of us.

Wait…Oklahoma? I forgot we were changing camp locations. I wanted to go to my familiar church campground! Selfish Candice protests.

So, what? It's a new campground, Calm Candice soothes, and the debate is over. I was looking forward to returning to our familiar campground, but it's okay. I've been to Oklahoma a few times with Dad on his speaking trips. There's no need to get worked up.

When we stop to eat, the reddish roads and hot wind make me feel like we're in the desert or something, not to mention the open plains lining the highway. Okay, maybe I'm over-analyzing every-thing. But it certainly *doesn't* feel like Missouri.

"I can't believe we're halfway to camp!" Jaclyn squeals once we return to the buses, propping up her feet on the seat in front of us.

"Me neither." I stare out the window. The bus is humid and full of chatter. I open the window to let in some air.

"You seem contemplative." She removes an earbud.

I dismiss her words with the wave of my hand. "Just tired." I prop up my feet next to hers and flash a smile. "This is gonna be the best camp ever!"

Frankly, my mind is spinning in a thousand directions. I asked God to give me a direct sign if we were going to move somewhere like Chicago or Florida, but the more I think about it, I'm not so sure that was a good idea. I mean, what if he does give me a blatant sign? Then I'd *have* to deal with it.

I just don't want any change in my life right now. Everything's just fine the way it is. I love my church, school, friends, and family. It's just too perfect to leave.

I guess I'm still playing the part of runaway Jonah.

This isn't Missouri. I grumble as the bus rolls into the camp-ground surrounded by red dirt and crookedly skinny trees with barely any leaves on them. I know I'm probably scrutinizing every-thing, but our Missouri campground has comfortable temperatures and rich, brown soil, unlike this desert land. I am tempted to feel the same homesick, vulnerable feeling I get when I am away from home, but I quickly shut it down. There's no need to get sentimental when it's supposed to be vacation time. I just have this ache in my heart, and it won't go away.

God, please work in my heart this summer camp, I pray, stepping off the bus.

You'll be pleased to know I have forgotten about what's going on in our family, and I've been focused on the camp games, late-night small groups, and powerful worship services…all until tonight. It's the third camp service altar time. I am standing in a huddle with my church friends, where everyone is exchanging prayers and wiping sensational tears. All except me.

Peeking around, I see Jaclyn wipe a tear away, and a new friend named Julie, who sleeps in our dorm, singing softly, and Jaclyn's friend Ava is praying over our circle. Closing my eyes once more, I sway and sniffle to sound like I am emotional. But I just can't wait to collapse on my bunkbed.

A hand taps my shoulder. It is my turn to pray. Drawing a deep breath, I begin with the usual words of group prayers (as a PK, this comes as naturally as singing "Happy Birthday").

"God, I thank you for—" my words hang in the air. All of my thoughts escape me. Everyone waits for me to keep praying, but I can't speak.

Oh, no. I feel that all-too-familiar whisper like in the Alabama church service. I don't like this. It is as evident as if God is in the middle of this circle, speaking in an audible voice. I can't escape it.

"Oh, God…" I shudder. Everyone's heads lift in bewilderment. Tears, real tears, stream down my flushed face. Jaclyn wraps her arms around me and prays I would be comforted. But I don't need comfort. I want to run out of the auditorium and away from God's voice.

"I'm so scared," I sob into Jaclyn's shirt. *"I'm so scared."*

You wanted an answer, God whispers bluntly. It is the same feeling I felt in the Alabama church service.

There's a change coming in our family.

I see this vision of myself walking down a checkered-floor school hallway surrounded by faces I've never seen before. My chin is up, and my eyes are fixed straight ahead.

I see myself in a cold, strange world.

The word *sacrifice* is written in my mind. Something is going to require personal sacrifice. *No, God!* I silently argue back.

You need to trust me, He says, calm and full of patience. *Trust me.*

But I don't want to go! I sniffle, wiping smeared mascara with my sleeve and pulling myself together.

I will be with you, He says, more real than the worship team's lyrics or a friend's audible voice. By now, I am doing the chattery cry where I can't breathe. Service has dismissed, and our huddle is broken by Julie.

"Is she okay?" I hear her whisper to Jaclyn.

"Let's go—I'm starving…" Ava yawns, and through watery eyes, I see the overhead lights brighten.

"We'll meet you at the snack shack," Jaclyn whispers in my ear, taking my Bible and journal and walking off with the crowd.

As I sit in the empty auditorium, I feel like I'm not supposed to share what God told me with my friends. I resolve to keep it to myself. This makes it seem like less of a concrete issue. Like something that only happened in my mind. But whether it was real or not, Comfortable Candice no longer exists.

The bus ride home is more than miserable. I feel absolutely sick.

"Want a Sour Patch Kid?" Jaclyn offers, reaching into the wrinkled bag of candy that somehow survived the whole week of camp.

"No, thanks." I curl up into a ball. If this is more than just a "camp high," what God spoke in service is about to wreck my life.

"Doesn't camp make you feel so…so…free?" Jaclyn smiles, staring at the roof of the bus. Her thick, caramel curls trail down the seat.

"Uh-huh," I answer, choking back tears. *I'm leaving Jaclyn.* The words play over and over. And then a greater reality hits: *I'm leaving everything!*

Maybe this isn't God, I rationalize, attempting to drown out the looming feeling in my mind. I reach for Jaclyn's earbud and focus on the lyrics of the Imagine Dragons song *Thunder*. To my dismay, we simultaneously pass a billboard promoting Oklahoma City's *Thunder* basketball team. *It's just a weird coincidence*, I reason, reaching for the bag of Sour Patch Kids. But it seems like everything is turning into one big coincidence.

"There's Been a Death"

"You won't believe what happened while you were gone." Mom tosses in the laundry detergent as I throw my camp swimsuit in the washing machine. I was just about to launch into all the weird coincidences I've had this summer—like what happened at camp—but she's beat me to the chase.

"This may sound strange, but four distinct prophecies have been spoken over our family by four different people." She widens her eyes.

There's your confirmation, I think to myself. "Who told you these things, psychic palm readers?" I screech in disbelief.

Mom laughs. "Sorry to disappoint, they weren't palm readers. First, while you've been at camp, we had lots of issues with the house—crazy issues—like the crawlspace under the house getting flooded, electrical lights flickering on and off, and then burning out, even glitches with the car…"

"Sounds evil."

"Not like that," she shakes her head. "One day, an electrician stopped by who said he wasn't even the employee supposed to come, but he felt like God was telling him to see us specifically. He said he wrestled with a word from God all weekend before coming to see us. There was strong spiritual opposition," she continues.

Now, this is getting eerie.

"He said that our family is called to do something big for God and that He is going to use our children."

"Pretty clear," I smirk.

"Just wait. While your dad was speaking at a camp, a random guy approached him with the *same type of prophecy*, along with two random ladies who told me the same thing without even realizing it. Something to do with the word 'initiative' and something 'beyond our normal circles.' It will cost us everything to get to this place..."

"Like a sacrifice?" I freeze, remembering how the word was tied to my vision at camp.

"Yes," she says slowly. "You know how God tests people—like with Abraham, He chose Isaac, Noah, He chose a boat, and Elijah, He chose a drought, rain, and fire. God chose a different test for each individual. The test is passed when you give everything to God. Some people who talked to us said it could mean leaving our family—or even each one of us specifically—giving up what we *thought* was our future, like living in Missouri for the rest of our lives. And the reward following the test the prophecies mentioned is having recognized and received His presence."

"Wow!" I stare at the eggplant-colored tiles on the laundry room floor, looking for anything in the world of remote familiarity. *I've never really noticed how the floor in here was purplish...*

"Are you listening?" Mom taps my shoulder.

"Uh-huh," I nod. "It's all just so hard to grasp. And I mean... prophecies? Real prophecies?"

"Cool, right?"

"Scary is more like it," I emphasize. "Besides...I don't know how to say this..."

"Just say it."

"I guess I'm mad at myself for not...not really seeing the need for *more* of God's presence. Like, we're already doing great here. I'm saved, you're saved, we go to church, there's a Bible verse hanging right there behind you..." I gesture to the *"Let all you do be done in love"* cross-stitch patterned frame on the wall. "My point is, why do we have to uproot everything to get more 'Christian'?"

"We're not moving to get more 'Christian,'" Mom's warm hand strokes my hair. "We're moving because we love God, and we sense

He is calling us to something more. We learn to trust His plan over ours. Don't you feel such joy by following God?"

"Not exactly." I curve my feet inward and cave my shoulders, retreating to my habitual stance of insecurity. Mom doesn't even correct my posture.

"Look, little Canzie. When you're a teenager, you're trying to figure out a lot of different things in your life, and spirituality is one of the trickiest."

"Tell me about it," I moan.

"But I believe God will show you there is *more* to walking with Him than you realize. As you grow up, it can be painful because it's unfamiliar. But true happiness is literally found in God."

"Well, it's not exactly butterflies and rainbows when God makes you leave friends and family." Goosebumps crawl up my arms.

"Oh." Mom reaches for her phone in her apron pocket. "That reminds me of another part of the prophecies someone spoke over us: *'Those you have chosen to surround yourselves with will not be allowed to enter this journey with you. This will become a new starting place for you.'* Isn't that interesting?!"

"More like depressing." I'm in a daze fixating on our clanky, twenty-year-old washing machine. "Mom, I'm so overwhelmed by all of this superstition."

"This isn't superstition. This is God in action. Though it is supernatural, it is still real. In fact, it's more real than anything we can see."

I allow her words to sink in for a period. Obviously, I have a lot of growing up to do in the area of faith and trust in God. But how do I begin?

Mom reads my thoughts. "Hardships will be your greatest teacher, like those tests I mentioned. And through those tests, you will be given the choice to either trust God or trust in yourself. No one can decide for you."

I stare hopelessly at the purple floor tiles, trying to process everything around me. "I didn't ask for this. I didn't ask for any of this!"

"None of us did." She reaches above the washing machine and opens her project cabinet, pulling out my old gingham dress amongst a wad of to-be-mended garments.

"I loved that dress."

"And you cried the day you outgrew it."

"Uh-huh…"

"But you tore it, again and again, playing outside. After a while, no matter how much you pleaded for me to let you keep it, the dress wouldn't fit. It was time to let go."

I wait for her analogy to spin full circle.

"So it is with our lives. The time comes when it's time to move on to something better."

"Sure," I say half-heartedly. "So, are there any specific prophecies about our new life in Chicago?"

Mom nods, the smile disappearing from her face. "Mm-mm…" She avoids my gaze.

"There some about me personally as well, how I will go through a season of…well, never mind." She slams the lid to the washing machine and looks me in the eyes. "The main point is, I think we should pray that God takes everything away that matters to us, so we will be completely unattached when we leave."

"You want everyone to *die*?"

"Oh no, Canzie." Innocence radiates off her face. "I just prayed for things like my job or your school you love so much—things that we are completely attached to—would not become so hard to leave. I think my prayer is already working…I mean, look at the house! It's like our little cottage is slowly dying away with all of the house repairs going on. And…" Mom hesitates midsentence, unsure of whether to express what is on her mind. "Have you looked outside yet?"

"No, why?"

Her sad expression makes me hesitant to look. She reaches for my hand, walking me out of the laundry room and to the window in the kitchen.

Almost immediately, I notice what's missing.

The Great Oak is gone.

The same tree we buried a treasure map in when I was a kid. The very tree in which we tried to carve our names, but it wouldn't work the bark, was too thick. My dear, loyal, colossal friend that provided shade over our playground and many imaginary games is missing. The tree that symbolized my untouchable childhood is missing.

The Great Oak is dead.

"No," I whisper.

"She was a faithful—" Mom comforts.

"He, Mom…it was a 'he'…"

"*He* was a faithful one."

This is the last straw. I stand gazing at the staple of my childhood, which is now replaced by a gaping hole of bleakness. Like a giant toothpick, he was bent over and cracked in two. *Not you too, old friend.* I touch the window.

"It was struck by lightning during a storm. We had a ceremony without you," Mom says in a mockingly official voice, as if it was silly to have a funeral for a tree.

Before following Mom into the laundry room, I breathe onto the window and draw a heart on it, so I can officially depart from him. *Goodbye, Great Oak.*

"Like I was saying," Mom continues, "if all of these things continue to happen—and they would have to be really crazy—then I would know God is calling us to move somewhere."

Crazy is an understatement. It's one thing for a tree to fall over dead, but what about the concrete staples in our lives, like losing our school? That's a tall order.

As I fall asleep, I cry over The Great Oak tree like it's my best friend. But after a while, I get tired of crying and think about what Dad said over dinner: *"I should have a tangible answer of what God wants us to do in mere weeks."*

What he probably means is that God *has* shown him what He wants us to do, but I am guessing it is such a broad direction that Dad is trying to translate in the physical sense. But in mere weeks? That's not a large chunk of time. What's it going to take for us to move, Mom losing her job? The Bricks kicking Kelly and me out of the group? Or maybe everyone drops out of school? We're talking about things in the 0.001 percentile happening. Mom's prayer for everything to fall apart sounds insane, but I don't necessarily blame her. In one way or another, I'm asking God for the same thing: absolute clarity.

My relatively normal life has evolved into one of those Twilight Zone shows. Except this one is going too far—it's turning into reality.

I think I should start writing down my dreams. Two nights ago, I dreamed The Great Oak turned into a hungry monster with lightning as fingers and chased us down the dark alleys of Chicago.

"Do you think it means something?" I asked Kelly while we brushed our teeth in the Jack and Jill bathroom we share in between our new rooms.

"Leave it to you and your dreams…of course, it doesn't! You're probably just overreacting to all of the prophecies you've heard," she said in a matter-of-fact voice. "But aren't the prophecies exciting?"

"That's one way to put it…" I rolled my eyes. These prophecies are too close to home—as in, close to stealing away my childhood bubble. Why can't it be a prophecy about my future husband or something?

Believe it or not, Mom's prayer for everything to fall apart is becoming a reality.

"You'll never believe this," Mom flung open the door to my room last night.

"You saw a Illinois license plate?" I threw out.

"No," she sighed, looking down at her phone. "Get ready for this…"

Kelly happened to be walking past my open door and popped in just as Mom said, "A messy drama happened at your school over the summer. All of the parents got involved, teachers were fired up—the entire school was in an uproar. Long story short, now we are relocating most of your class—the Bricks—to a different co-op location. I'm so sorry!"

"What?" I managed to say in a raspy voice. *This is ridiculous!* We aren't going to go meet at the same church location we've met at since junior high? What is this, some middle school drama?

"…and that's not all," Mom continued. "Uncle Austin and his family are moving away because of his job. They leave next month!"

"You've got to be kidding!"

"No way!" Kelly protested.

"Oh, and don't get me started about work…" Mom seethed. "I won't go into all of the details, but I'm leaving my writing job."

"Seriously?"

"It's for the best," Mom said quickly, "But I didn't expect everything to change like that," she snapped her fingers. "Girls, something is happening—in your lives and in mine—and now is not the time to close your eyes and hope everything works out."

"You've been ignoring my texts for the past week!" Sophia screeches on the phone. I happened to see her call before heading out for a run with Charlie.

"It's been kind of crazy at home," I say, which is a total understatement. To be perfectly honest, I've reread her texts a thousand times, but I'm too preoccupied to respond. August has just begun, and you'd think it was the end of the world or something. Dad hasn't revealed his decision yet on what's happening in the family, but he has been frequenting his speaking trips—specifically to Chicago—so if that's not a sign, what is?

Mom's been rampaging the attic and garage, getting rid of practically everything that wasn't used in the past month. Kelly checked out from the library a stack of Christian books about the end of the world. Bria and Allison, the preteens of the family, have been moping around the house like they've just been given a death sentence. And so, being the only one at home with a sound mind, I am automatically the babysitter for Angel and Jordan. Just the way I envisioned spending my last few days of summer.

"I was wondering if you wanted to go to Silver Dollar City with me tomorrow," Sophia asks, referring to the amusement park that we enjoy together.

"I'd love to, but—" I begin.

"Pick you up at eight?"

"Actually, I'll have to check with my mom." I walk Charlie down the driveway and look back at Mom, who's currently covered in sweat and working in the garage. "She's been tied up with a lot of house things."

"Okay, just let me know," Sophia says graciously. I picture her taking off her visor and debriefing after a long day of work. I'm thankful she hasn't asked me why I've been so preoccupied these past few weeks, though my heart longs to tell her.

Of course, Mom would probably be fine with me going to Silver Dollar City because all she's thinking about is *moving-moving-moving*. But then I think about how the kids might need my help because Dad's away. I consider texting Sophia and telling her I can't meet up because of that, but then I remember how I might only have a few more days as a normal Missouri kid before moving to Chicago.

So, the next morning, we drive down the forty-five-minute highway to the amusement park in hopes of having a day of pleasure. I roll down the window and let my hair fly in the wind. I'm trying really hard to enjoy myself—I'm even cheerily wearing my 1950s white, pointy sunglasses to show I am my usual quirky self. I don't want Sophia to know I'm a total mess on the inside, and I'm definitely not ready to grieve aloud.

Thankfully, I do enjoy the day and even convince Sophia to ride one of the daredevil roller coasters with me. We end the day with lemonade slushies and a shared potato stick on our way out of the park, laughing as old friends and young teenagers. On the drive home, I contemplate how I will tell people about moving to Chicago...*if* it ends up evolving into something real. You've got to plan for the worst-case scenario because the last thing you want is to be caught off guard when your parents make the decision. Because one day, you might wake up and the decision is made—whether you like it or not.

"The Announcement"

I am balancing my steamy plate of chicken as I approach the table. The smell of hot barbeque makes my mouth water. I sit down in my usual spot—the tucked-away corner seat on the right side of Mom. It is another ordinary summer dinner with the family, except right now, everyone's on pins and needles to hear if we're moving. Nothing major.

Dad arrived home from work an hour past his usual time and retreated to his office for a time of prayer. Then he texted all of us and said he had an important matter to discuss at dinner. Would he really reveal the decision right here, right now?

Mom sat in her closet all afternoon with the lights off eating dark chocolate, and Jordan was running around in his underwear, so I resorted to telling him stories about a little stick figure named Adam. The story followed Adam learning how to get dressed in the morning. Jordan praised the story until I erased the drawing board and said, "let's be like Adam."

I eventually gave up and ran outside in defeat, but then I saw The Great Oak's gaping hole and quickly retreated to my room to journal but was met by a smell that reminds me of expired broccoli mixed with paint—and it's not my laundry this time. The cottage, which has been in repair mode for the past two weeks with creepy worker guys emerging from every room in the house, was sprayed with a skunk last night. I think it crawled under the house when the workers were painting hallways and redoing the crawlspace.

Anyways, now I can't even breathe because of the stench. *Can things get any worse?*

"Achem," Dad clears his throat to talk.

Yes, it can, I think to myself, jumping in my chair.

Dad's face is red. He seems excited. As kitchen chairs screech across the hardwood floor, Dad asks, "How is everyone doing?" and I know he is trying to get everyone's attention, but this is the wrong question to ask when six girls are at the table.

"I got to go swimming today!" Angel blurts out. "But Jordan took my floaty."

"I did not!" Jordan retorts. "I got that floaty for my birthday!"

"Jordan, you should have let Angel use it for a while," Allison corrects. "Oh, Dad, I learned a new choreography at ballet. And I've almost conquered my first pirouette!" she crosses her fingers.

"I got coffee with Elia and…" says Bria.

"So that's why you smell like coffee!" Kelly interjects.

"I had lunch with Vicki today. You remember Vicki—used to be across the street?" Mom comments to Dad, who barely hears her. I remain silent as usual, observing everyone excitedly share their daily events. I eventually scoot back my chair and stare down at Charlie, who thinks I'm his real mom.

"What did you do today?" I whisper. He licks my hand. Sometimes he acts like he's worked his tail off, but all he did was eat, sleep, and chase a few birds away from The Great Oak's burial site. Hard life, I know.

Am I insignificant to God, like how Charlie's problems mean nothing to me? I think.

I've been thinking a lot these days. I am starting to doubt my faith more than ever. It's like I've never truly owned my personal belief in God until now. *And this is just another deep problem added to my list…* My mind spirals into a black hole.

"Achem," Dad clears his throat, attempting to gain control of the high-pitched dinner table conversations directed by six females. If this didn't happen every night, I might try to do something. But this is totally normal, and so more minute's pass of mindless girl

chatter. Finally, Dad finishes his plate and stands up to get fruit salad for dessert. No one notices he leaves, nor when he sits down again.

"So," he tries again, his dark features solemn. "I received another call from a pastor in Chicago. They want our whole family to come back and spend a few days in the area."

Oh, that's no big deal. I chew a thick piece of chicken and nod at his words. Dad doesn't want to move. Just like me. Nothing to worry about.

"Why is Dad so serious?" Kelly whispers in my ear.

It is evident Dad is holding back something, and he doesn't know how to say it. I turn my eyes to Mom, who looks solemn herself, except for the dark chocolate smudge on her cheek.

"Everyone want to play a game?" Dad approaches the subject in a different way. "I'll ask a question, and everyone can say their *quick* response."

I walk over to the countertop and scoop a spoonful of fruit salad into a bowl, taking my eyes off the table game. *Blah…blah…blah.* I tune out the words. This isn't good. Dad has a way of making serious things fun, which makes me wary. I am going off past experiences— like when I was ten years old and Dad had to deliver the news about another serious announcement, he played this exact game.

"What if we moved to Chicago?" he throws out lightheartedly. I continue to stand at the counter, eating my fruit. Mom's face twitches. She knows some kind of secret. *Oh, you're just overanalyzing everyone.* I shake off the skepticism in my mind.

"I'll go for fun!" Angel agrees on the whim of the moment.

"No way!" Bria cries out, slamming her fist on the table.

"Whatever God wants us to do," Kelly comments in a spiritual tone.

"What if that's what God *is* calling us to do?" Mom adds to Dad's question.

"But He never said that…did He?" I finally chime in, standing on my tiptoes to add to my confidence. "Didn't you say God was letting you discern what the prophecies meant in the physical sense?" I remind him.

Dad finishes his glass of water. "Partially. But what if He is leading me to one decision over another?" He sits up straight. "So, everyone, if I *did* feel like God was calling us to move somewhere, how would you feel about it?"

"Well, if it's for sure God telling us to move somewhere, of course, I would go," I mumble dejectedly. *Can't they wait until I'm out of the house to move?* I think, scrunching up my nose.

But then I remember the vision I had at camp and how the pastor's words hit me so strongly that there was no denying it was supernatural. God has me involved in this charade, whether I like it or not. And, though I hate to say it, it is one step away from becoming official.

August 22nd

"We have a Gibbons family announcement." Mom clasps Dad's hand in the living room. The previous time this happened, Mom and Dad announced we were getting a new baby brother. So, this could be an adoption party. Or maybe we just won the lottery, and we're about to fly out to the Bahamas. Or maybe I actually have a twin sister, and they're about to bring her out. Maybe her name is Shmandice, and she's hiding in that closet over there…

I wish.

"I knew it. We're moving," Bria throws out flatly.

"Shh!" Mom says in a mix of irritation and excitement.

I know where this meeting is headed. After two months of questions, prophecies, hopes, and fears, Mom and Dad have finally come to a decision.

Don't tell me—we are moving to Chicago.

I wish I could try my persuasion skills like I did with the popsicle, or to have a dog, or to finally get my own room—try to convince Mom and Dad that there's nothing to consider, that we are okay right where we are—but I can't ignore the facts. *I* heard God speak to me in Alabama. *I* had a vision at camp. Now everything has led to this moment, and it's the moment that will mark the rest of my life.

"Your daddy and I have been praying about where God might be leading our family…" Mom continues.

"I can't believe we're actually having this conversation," I whisper to Kelly, who is holding her phone positioned to video. I gather everyone feels this way after watching Angel work up tears in her eyes in advance of the announcement being revealed.

"We know everyone is anxiously awaiting the final decision." Dad has a stressed smile on his face. He has reassured us that his decision wouldn't affect this year's school semester, but I'm not clueless. *Any* major decision—whether it's Chicago or Niagara Falls—affects the rest of high school for me—no Bricks at school, no more weekends with my grandparents, no more life! And the worst part is the fact that everyone's going along with it like it's logical. *Logical? Leaving everything you know to go after an unknown call from God?*

Mom whispers something in Dad's ear and then turns to us. "The three options are: moving to Chicago, moving to Oklahoma City, or staying in Ozark," she says, but we already know that. I've even drawn up a chart with pros and cons for each of the options, and it's been taped to the fireplace mantle for the past week (though I've had to rip it down whenever someone comes over). Here it is:

Chicago	Oklahoma City	Ozark
- Windy weather	- Red dirt roads	- BEST TOWN EVER
- Not as familiar with the church	- Somewhat familiar with the church	- FRIENDS + FAMILY
- Really far away		- HOME IS HERE
	- Closer to home than Chicago	

Obviously, choice #3 is idealistic. And it's not like it's totally out of the question to stay here, either. One thing I haven't talked to anyone—and I mean anyone—about is how I'm genuinely scared to move to such big cities…not that it's NYC or anything, but because

I've been raised in such a small, protected town that's thirty minutes away from the nearest Target, it would definitely feel like it. *It's not like Dad's moving away without you*, I remind myself, hoping it brings even the tiniest amount of comfort. But maybe it's not Dad that makes me feel better; maybe it's home itself. My comfortable, cozy cottage home. My perfect friends. My perfect church. My perfect life.

"Is it hot in here for you?" I ruffle my tee shirt. Kelly shakes her head. I need air. I need water. But as I stand to get some, everyone's chants fill the room.

"Ozark! Ozark! Ozark!" the girls sing.

"THREE, TWO, ONE," Mom and Dad countdown.

No! Not yet! I haven't had time to think! I race back into the room and fumble for my phone, pressing the recording button just in time to hear the words that will shape my life forever.

"We are moving to Oklahoma!" Mom and Dad announce in unison.

Wait a minute…Oklahoma?!

Everyone erupts in screams and cheers, hugging one family member after another. Charlie flies up in the air as I jump to my feet, half in protest, half in disbelief. No one knows whether to laugh, cry, or stay solemn, so screaming is the only option. Well, if this is one of those hidden camera TV shows, I need to speak up.

"You can come on out, guys," I joke aloud. But my words are drowned in the tears and screams of those around me. And it's sinking in how monumental this moment is.

"We're going to New Life Church in Oklahoma City," Dad explains. "Our good friends, the Jacksons, are pastors there, and we are going to serve alongside them." Letting out a deep breath, Dad wraps his arms around Mom. "This is it, Case."

I try to laugh it off like I usually do in serious moments, but I can't. I'm speechless.

It is happening. It is actually happening.

I rub my eyes in disbelief. The decision is made. There's no need to worry, guess, or disregard all of the curious feelings I've wrestled throughout summer.

When will it happen? What will our house be like? Would I be happy in Oklahoma? A zillion questions flood my mind, and it doesn't help Mom and Dad are clueless, too.

But here is the blatant truth: The Gibbons' family, perfectly settled in the town of Ozark, Missouri, is moving away to the red-dirt-roads state.

I make eye contact with Dad and smile. Even though I wouldn't have picked his decision for myself, I trust him.

It's official. Candice Gibbons is moving to...*Oklahoma!*

"The Twilight Zone"

I thought my life couldn't get any worse. I was wrong.

"I'm having surgery?" I repeated in disbelief.

Here I am, finding out we're moving to Oklahoma and just weeks away from starting my sophomore year of high school, only to hear I have to face every teen's nightmare: the dreaded wisdom teeth surgery. I am beginning to wonder if this really is some kind of prank—like I'm an anonymous victim on a hidden camera TV show, and a group of people is sitting in a studio laughing at me.

I don't think I can take another unexpected crisis right now. Seriously, I just want to curl up in a ball and hide in my laundry basket. And I totally *would* curl up in my laundry basket...if it weren't so full of clothes. The timing of this couldn't be more perfect. It was bad enough I was preparing to drop the news that I'm *moving* when I walk into school, now I'm going to look like a chipmunk. As if my life wasn't already falling apart. This is just great.

Part of me wants to reschedule the surgery for, I don't know, sometime in Oklahoma. After all, won't that be in another lifetime? I'm not totally serious; I'm sure life will be great and all. But maybe I could postpone the surgery for the day in Oklahoma when nobody knows me...

"Sorry, this is the only option," Mom told me the night before. "Besides, we don't want to wait too long. The dentist said your wisdom teeth have got to come out now."

And so, here I am, grudgingly throwing on sweatpants and a camp tee shirt before tossing some soft snacks in a drawstring bag and stomping out to the car at 5:30 a.m.

I hope Mom doesn't video me post-surgery—you know, when you're all loopy and unfiltered. *I should've put on makeup.* I wonder, knowing it is totally possible she will video me.

I try to think about something soothing, but nothing comes to mind. Childhood seems like a lifetime ago. Has it only been two months since I sat on the porch swing looking at The Great Oak planning my summer? I feel a hundred years older.

My friends already think I've gone off the deep end: I can barely say hello to Jaclyn at church because I'm afraid I'll start crying, and then she'll ask what's wrong, and then I'll have to blame it on something other than moving...like how I'm grieving the loss of The Great Oak, which will sound so immature. I guess that's what grief does to people. One minute you're normal, the next minute you're not.

I could focus on home today. I can remember all of the happy memories of running in the field, having picnics under the tree, and tending to the worm farm I made down by the cow pasture. I can focus on memories of being homeschooled: switching costumes five times a day, marching around the neighborhood with instruments, biking to the creek and throwing rocks in the lake, making homemade snickerdoodle cookies, and singing to *The Sound of Music...*

Oh, great. Just thinking of home makes me want to cry. The worst thing I can do to myself is to be emotional today. *Come on, Candice. Pull it together!*

"Right this way," a college-aged nurse escorts me to the sticky dentist chair. I observe the dental tools on a sterile tray that looks like torture devices, and I quickly notice the IV hookup to my right and an elderly-looking nurse smiling sinisterly beside it. As three nurses pry me with all of the medical wires, tubes, scanners, anesthesia, and who knows what else, the drowsiness begins, and I am left with my own thoughts.

There's a prophecy about your family...
A prophecy over your life...
Our lives...prophecy over our lives...
We're moooooving to Oklahoma...
Oklahoma...Oklahoma...Okla—
Sinking slowly into darkness, I fall unconscious.

Where am I? What's going on?
I open my eyes to a room of blurry brown chairs. I squint my eyes and sit up a little straighter in what I realize is a wheelchair, and I realize I am sitting by myself in a very dated '80s-designed lobby with purple wallpaper and fake foliage. I feel a cold tear trickle down my cheek, and I soon realize it's blood when I smudge it with my hand.

"Shmushmushmush..." I hear Mom's mumbled voice behind me, probably talking to a nurse. I glance up at the grandfather clock beside the women's bathroom door and realize the surgery time passed by swiftly. Apparently, I've only been here two hours, but it might as well be two years. Why am I so confused? Is this another dimension?

Oh, don't try to sort out life's problems now, Candice, I tell myself. I'll be home soon, and thank goodness everything will be back to normal. Oklahoma is just a part of this dream, so if I can tolerate it a little longer, soon I'll wake up and be outside beside The Great Oak, laughing and playing in the fall leaves.

But on my way home, the dream still hasn't ended, and all of these words fly out of my mouth, and I can't stop them:

Where even is Oklahoma?
Why is my face swollen?
I don't want to leave!
I want ice cream. Peppermint ice cream.

Mom is videoing me, but I'm so high I don't really care. I shake my head back and forth and groan in anguish to cope the rest of the way home. Because this is only a bad dream, and someday I am going to wake up. Someday.

Wake up! Wake up! I moan. My eyes open to a white sheet over my head. *Am I dead?*

It's silent all around me. And then I hear a bird tweet—no—two birds are chirping.

So, this is what Heaven is like…

"She's awake," I hear Annie whisper…or at least, I think it is her.

"You're here too?" I whisper in disbelief. At least we're both safe in heaven together.

Suddenly, a dark shadow hovers over my face. I try to scream, but my mouth is full of what tastes like toilet paper. The shadow, which I now realize is an arm, is grabbing hold of the white sheet and slowly pulling it away from my face. The light is so bright I cover my eyes with my hands.

Immediately feeling liquid, I slowly pull my hands away from my face and gasp. *"My hands are covered in blood!"*

"You're what?" the voice giggles, and I see Annie walk closer. I realize my words sounded like *"my ham ah hover in bluh."*

Annie dips a washcloth in a bowl of water and wipes the blood off my face. "Just rest, Candy Cane. You've had a big three days."

Three days? Surely, I haven't been here for three days.

I muster all the strength I have to prop myself up in bed. The room is spinning, and my cheeks are throbbing with pain. My skin is glistening with sweat. My mouth tastes acidy and dry all at the same time.

"Ice. I nee ice." I point to my mouth. Annie pulls the sheets up from my stomach and hands me a blue ice pack that wormed its way there while I was sleeping.

"Hanks," I say, the icepack plopping on the left side of my face like a sizzling hot iron. As it does, my eyes roll back in my head. I then feel a rush of cool air blow in, and I hear the door close.

I am all alone now. I don't see Mom. I don't see Dad. I don't feel God. I am completely vulnerable.

"She's fevered. Her antibiotics aren't working. We need to get her to the doctor." I toss and turn as Mom's words echo in the air.

"Casey, it's been a week. Do you think something's wrong?" another voice says.

"There has to be. She can barely talk."

"Ow...*ow!*" I cry in anguish. The sounds of drills and of scissors clipping mixed with one of those things that sucks all of the water out of your mouth ring in my ears.

It's like a nightmare come true. I'm back in the dentist's chair.

"Just be still." The same sinister nurse holds my arms down.

Something's cutting open the stitches on the right side of my mouth. It doesn't feel right. Someone has to stop this! Tears are streaming down my face, and I try to cry out for Mom to save me, but I have a handful of gauze stuffed in my mouth. It feels like I'm having surgery without the anesthesia.

"I'll go! I'll go!" I cry out to God. "I won't run from you or Oklahoma anymore. Just make them stop hurting me!"

Blood trickles down my throat. I feel the doctor push a hard bracket into the hole where my tooth was. I wish I could fall asleep and escape the pain, but I can't.

This is not a dream.

"Oh, you poor baby!" Gigi laments on the phone. "Your Aunt Angela and I have been praying for you like crazy."

"Hank ew," I mumble beneath the wad of gauze, looking over at the flowers beside my bed our pastor sent over from the church. If only flowers could make everything better. My whole left cheek is swollen into an abnormally large purple knot. I can barely eat, drink, or even breathe properly. Can it get any worse?

I shouldn't think like that, because it probably *can* get worse… though I can't imagine how. I've been dragging myself to the doctor for weeks, and every time, it's the same horrible routine: cut, drain, stitch. Worst part? I am awake every time he breaks open the incision and drains out the infection. It hurts so bad I can't help but cry as blood goes out everywhere; Mom leaves the room, and I dig my nails in the palm of my hand to distract me from the pain.

I am merely days away from the first day of school, and my face looks three times the size of its actual dimensions. Diana and Sophia have offered to come to visit, but I'd rather not scare them at this point in time; we only have so many more days together. I don't want their lasting image of me to be Candice, XXL version.

As I lay in bed and contemplate everything that is wrong in my life, Mom walks in with shocked eyes and a phone to her ear. "We picked the wrong doctor."

The doctor who did my surgery has been inappropriately operating the way he drained my infection. Instead of putting me to sleep, reopening the incision, and fully draining my infection, he would cut open my wound to squeeze out the infection little by little…while I was awake. *And I wonder why my mouth isn't healing…*

"She'll need a completely new operation where we will have to drain all of the infection and redo some of the construction," says the new doctor, prying at my sore gums. My face is like a balloon, my cheeks are like that of a giant pufferfish, and my soul grieves as if I have already moved. But thank God I have a *normal* oral surgeon now. The only other good thing is, at least I can lock myself in my own room. But even then, we're moving.

The spiritual side of Candice is itching to realize God's purpose behind this. I think He is stretching me to push through an unprecedented situation—a cold, lonely, and lengthy season lying in bed drenched in tears—before an even greater trial: moving to Oklahoma. Thank goodness I surrendered my Jonah feelings about running from God's will. But now, I have to follow through with my promise to obey Him.

One thing is certain: I am not the selfish teenager I was at the beginning of summer. Though I've believed in God since I was a child, it isn't until now I am faced with the toughest decision in the world: surrendering my life to Him. It almost feels like I am choosing between giving my heart to Christ or not—but for *real* this time. Like, actually serving Him with all of my heart.

Well, from how things are looking right now, God's plan is horrible. I dream endless dreams of repeatedly opening my mouth for surgery and telling the Bricks we are moving. I wake up every morning and cry happy tears if I'm able to open up my swollen cheeks enough to eat, or sad tears if I can't. I'm on so many medications for swelling and pain. I'm constantly groggy and drugged up. Still, I'm *not* going to miss the first day of my sophomore year. I guess it's better to knock out the embarrassment on the front end rather than later. Besides, it's my last, first day with the Bricks'.

Mom said I'll be having another operation next week to fully drain the infection. And as much as I am dreading the whole surgical process, I am thankful to finally have the right doctor. Just two months ago, immature Candice would be whining, crying, and pouting over how unfair life is just because she had to drive to Alabama. But now, I have greater battles to fight. Yes, I will have been bedridden for two weeks with two surgeries, three different medications while surviving on chicken noodle soup, but stubborn Candice doesn't cave in under pressure.

Now, here's one Bible character you don't hear much about in sermons, I think, flipping open the Book of Job in the Old Testament before I go to sleep. I had read Job a few times before, like when I got pneumonia last winter. Job was a man who experienced the worst of circumstances. He lost his family, money, and health yet still trusted God. And because he continued to seek God, he was given twice as many blessings as before, and his seemingly endless trials didn't last forever.

I can relate to his pain—especially with the *Big Move* at my fingertips. I'm mad at God with Job. I'm angry I have to leave home. I thought I was going to stay here forever.

But at this moment, I have a choice to make: Will I trust God and follow His will for my life, even if I don't like it? Or will I follow my own desires and ignore all of this spiritual stuff? Well, I can't ignore the supernatural world. So, my choice is obvious, but not easy.

I'm not sure how this is going to play out, but I am tired of being Jonah and pretending everything is normal when God has spoken to our family and my parents have made a decision. And from what I've read about people in the Bible like Job, they were always blessed as a result of their obedience. I guess I am choosing to trust God above my own judgment. So, even though the light at the end of the tunnel isn't visible, I am going to trust him with my future. I'm not going to butter up my current situation and call it easy; I have so many questions and very few answers. But when I make up my mind about something, there's no turning back.

Mark my words: Candice Gibbons has accepted God's call to move to Oklahoma, no matter the cost.

"Wrestling"

"We need a lawyer," Aunt Angela says after I explain what happened. She scrapes chopped vegetables straight from Poppy's Garden off a cutting board and into the sizzling skillet stir-fry.

"That's what I told her, Daddy!" Gigi adds, stirring the pot of butter beans. I wish I could smell the rich scent of farm cooking, but ever since my second surgery with the new oral surgeon, I've lost my sense of smell. Mom said it would pass, but that's what she said about the swelling…and it's still here.

"You said the doctor was illegally operating?" Aunt Angela asks.

"I wouldn't call it malpractice," I soften the accusation. "He was just putting me through, er…unnecessary pain."

"Unbelievable," she shakes her head disapprovingly.

"I say we take this to court," says Poppy, walking into the kitchen with a tray of sizzling hamburgers. Out of all my grandparents, Poppy and I are the most alike—not just in appearance, but in our personalities. When it comes to delivering justice, we are unwavering leaders.

The hard part is, I don't have the energy nor the desire to go to court right now.

"I'm fine, really," I assure everyone in the kitchen. "I'm with a good doctor now, so there's nothing to worry about."

No one is convinced.

"Really!" I repeat. And then my phone buzzes. "Oh, I have to go take my steroids," I excuse myself away from the suspicious glares of my family members. I couldn't be more grateful that they care about my well-being. Having family members to back you up in a crisis is priceless.

As I think about it, what I *really* want is a court case against moving to Oklahoma. With all of my passionate aunts, uncles, and grandparents on my side, I'm sure I could win.

No, Candice. You're going because God called you, remember? I remind myself, popping the steroid into my mouth and gulping down water. The taste of this medicine reminds me of those bitter days in bed with the white sheets. Oh, those white sheets. All of those sleepless nights covered in sweat. Thank God those days are behind me.

Still—and don't be mad at me—but I kind of see my decision to move to Oklahoma quite differently now that I am not on pain medication. It's not as if I'm going back on my word—like I made a rash promise in a desperate moment—but I'm considering the well-being of my extended family. *Is this really a good change?*

"Annie's about to pull up. Are you ready to go?" Mom says after dinner as I finish vacuuming the floor.

"I forgot it's Sunday!" I drop the vacuum in excitement. In just two days, I'll be detached from my blissful freshman summer and be sucked into the world of academics, so I better enjoy life while I can…not that this summer was blissful, but school is going to mount the load of pressure I'm feeling with my mouth pain. Thankfully (or dreadfully, depending on how you look at it), Mom and Dad said we only have one more day of holding in the news about moving to Oklahoma. Then we can tell anyone and everyone what's happening, and maybe it will make me feel better (or worse).

"Well, put the vacuum away because she will be here any minute!" Mom says with a smile. I'm not even going to think about Oklahoma tonight. I won't let anything spoil my time at Annie's house.

As I slam the door to the cleaning closet, I hear her high-pitched horn in the driveway.

"Remember not to say anything about—"

"I know, I know. Don't say anything about moving to Oklahoma until tomorrow!" I yell, running out the door. It feels like I'm playing a game of some sort. I've never had to keep a secret like this. It's partly exciting, partly frightening. And sooner or later, it won't be a secret.

The sun is setting, and the air is warm and humid. Crickets chirp in the distance, along with the mooing of cows and clacking of chickens at Mr. Coggins' farm. It's a cool Missouri sunset, and I don't even care that I'm barefoot and my hair is in a sloppy ponytail because right now, I'm just a kid going to my grandma's house.

Annie honks one more time just for fun while I'm *clearly* walking to the car, which makes me jump. "Hey there, kiddo," she greets me as I jump in the front seat. The windows are rolled down, and the Beach Boys are singing. "You ready to party?" she says, putting on her purple sunglasses.

"Oh yeah!" I turn up the music. We speed down the smooth, back roads and sing to our hearts' content. As we pull into their suburban neighborhood hidden beneath overgrown willow trees, I let my arm dangle out the window and breathe in the Missouri air. It pains me to hold in the news about moving. *Not going to think about it. Not going to think about it...*

"Your mouth looks better!" Papa acknowledges in a tone that's half-convincing.

"Thanks," I rub my cheek. It still feels like I have a ping pong ball in the side of my face. But I'd rather look like a pufferfish than have plastic surgery.

"Any big plans for this school year, *sophomore?*" Annie cuts her plate of baked ham into bite-sized triangles while Papa washes up from work. I look longingly at the feast before me, quite unlike Mom's last try at chicken casserole. But as hungry as I am, my mouth is beginning to throb. I play with my mashed potatoes and search for the right words.

"I, ugh, I want to have a big sixteenth birthday party!" I announce out of nowhere.

Oh, goodness. It hasn't hit me until now that I should probably be planning my *last* birthday in Missouri. That's crazy! I've had the same style of birthday parties since I was six: carnival games, talent shows, costumes—you name it, I did it. I guess my birthday's going to die when I move to Oklahoma. No more friends. No more donuts. No more fun.

"Say, there's nothing more I like than a good party! Honey, why don't you get out the ice cream carton?" Papa exclaims.

"Oh, Robert," Annie playfully slaps his shoulder. "What does your mom think about the party?"

"I haven't asked her yet. Mom and Dad are busy with the church in Okla—" I bite my tongue.

"New Life Church, isn't it? Is it that one Oklahoma church your dad speaks at from time to time?" Papa interrupts.

"Uh…er, yes, sir. Dad's there right now. It's just his typical speaking trip," I say nonchalantly. *Yeah, more like picking out our future house right now.*

"My word," Annie mutters in her Alabama accent. "He sure has been going there a lot."

"You're not *moving*, are you?" Papa freezes his lifted fork piled with green beans, emphasizing *moving* like it is a bad word. Before I can answer, Annie beats me to the question.

"Course they're not, Robert! Her daddy wouldn't move his family from Missouri. I heard him say he wouldn't unless God told him to…" she trails off.

We finish the night, as usual, conversating in politics, and by request of Papa, scooping into the strawberry cheesecake ice cream carton. I try to look like I'm not hiding anything, but I'm sure my blank face gives it away. I've always been immune to showing my emotions in the most inopportune circumstances. *No more Cruisin' Tuesdays. No weekends at Annie's.* What else am I going to miss? The fact I have to shut up one of the biggest secrets I've ever carried eats at me like a worm in my stomach.

Just one more day.

I wake up this morning covered in sweat. For a minute, I let out a sigh and tell myself the past month was some kind of bad dream, and now everything will be back to normal.

My navy-blue journal is lying open in front of me. I must've fallen asleep during an entry. *If this is all a dream, I won't have anything written about moving. Maybe, just maybe...* I reach for my diary and bite my lip.

Alas, it's true. I'm moving to Oklahoma.

I imagine the Bricks' faces on the first day of school when I tell them that Kelly and I are moving away. This is going to be one miserable school year...if I ever live to see it.

I try sitting up in bed, but my core aches like I'm fresh out of stomach surgery. I think it's because I stayed up nearly half the night crying myself to sleep, but then I had to shut it down because my mouth started bleeding. I remember crying about losing our home, friends, and family, and eventually, my tears led to my dog Charlie dying, which came out of nowhere. Charlie isn't even sick. I think I'm just overly emotional. Maybe if I dump some cold ice on my face and have a good breakfast, I'll feel better.

Once I throw on some shorts and an old camp T-shirt, I hazily walk into the kitchen to find it empty and silent. I walk over to the counter and find a note in Annie's handwriting.

Going to work. Will be at your house later tonight.
Have fun with Diana!

—Annie

71

Oh, great. I forgot today is the day I start working my way down the list of beloved friends and family members and telling them about the *Big Move.* The most life-altering day of my fifteen years on planet earth. What if I come across too emotional? Or too insensitive? And the worst of all, what if they think I'm only joking?

I sit down with a bowl of Papa's low-cholesterol honey cereal and rack my brain about how I am going to tell Diana the news. Diana is a true country Missouri girl who lives on a ranch and loves riding her mules. We're probably going to ride tonight, so I need to prepare how I am going to say it—even *when* I am going to say it. It's not as if I can just blurt it out and expect us to enjoy the rest of our evening. I sink in my chair at the thought and try not to cry again. It is sickening to think this is just the beginning of the long, sad journey telling everyone I love that I'm leaving forever—I probably won't even set foot in Missouri again once I board the moving truck. I better get a good look at my surroundings.

I glance outside and notice the August sun beaming down on the old oak trees. It's a beautiful day, which doesn't match my cloudy emotions. I wish it were stormy and dark, and there were sirens and people on the streets with signs reading, *"Stay in Missouri! Stay in Missouri!"* in front of my parents' windows. Maybe that would make them change their minds…

A bird flies into the window and jerks me back to reality. No, protesting wouldn't do the trick. We would need a prophecy telling us to stay in Missouri or something of that sort. And I almost want to pray for one, but that would feel like a contradiction since I prayed for clarity, and then God revealed we are moving to Oklahoma. Can't get more clear than that.

I'm really in no mood for summer activities, but outside does look inviting. I don't go running that often, especially since the doctor told me not to do much physical activity ever since I had the foot surgery where they broke bones in both of my feet and repositioned them with screws. As if bad health follows me, I also have an autoimmune disorder called POTS, which basically means I am extremely lightheaded when I sit and stand or do anything active in the heat. But, even if it sounds ironic, running feels so natural. I'm not exactly a sprinter, but I can cover a bit of land with my strides. And in my home neighborhood, along with Annie's neighborhood, there are several hills and trails for nice morning jogs. I think I'll go for a run and sort through my emotions. Because today, the truth comes out.

"Breaking News"

Diana gallops through the field on her mule, Banjo, her black curls bouncing with every stride. The scenic prairie scattered with hay reminds me of an old western movie, and the wind smells like Missouri's earthy soil, along with a typical farm pasture stench and a cool hint of autumn's near arrival. I am trotting Diana's mule, Apache, and contemplating when I should tell Diana about the *Big Move*.

Oh, Diana. My true dearest friend.

We weren't always close. In middle school, Diana was the proper, intelligent girl, while I was the creative leader of the classroom. Though we competed for the leader role in middle school, high school leveled us out as good friends. We laugh now at our old rivalry, and we like to pretend to be Anne and Diana from *Anne of Green Gables*.

Far ahead, Diana slows Banjo and stops at the fence gate.

"You're riding slow," she tells me, catching her breath and grinning. I trot Apache over to the fence and lean down on his mane.

"Apache and I were deep in thought," I say, questioning if it is time to reveal the news.

"Want to ride in front of my house by the road?" she asks, but my mind is elsewhere. The wind blows a lengthy gust, and we remain silent for a brief moment. Diana lifts her deep brown eyes to my teary blue eyes, studying my countenance.

"Is there something you need to tell me?" she whispers.

She's onto me, like any best friend.

"It's kind of hard to begin," I stutter, avoiding eye contact. All of a sudden, Missouri feels like a sort of heaven, a secure, comforting, and familiar place of wholesome living. I clutch Apache's rein and gulp back tears.

Things will never be the same after I utter these words, I realize, which doesn't help me present the news any easier. I feel rather awkward and uncomfortable, especially because Diana is the first person I am telling.

"Diana, there's something our family has been praying about this summertime..." I mumble, trying to remain steady. "And... well, God has given our family clear direction over our future." *In Oklahoma, that is,* I say to myself, finally looking at Diana. She squints her eyes in confusion. It is probably better for me to just spit it out than drag out this bitterly sad conversation.

"I, well, God has called us to...move...to...Oklahoma!" I spill in one very long breath.

"Oh, Candice," she gasps, staring at me. I wait earnestly for a heartfelt response to comfort my own panicking emotions. Still, I realize she must process it as I did.

Diana remains silent.

I try to think of something more to say, but I can't. It feels too much like when Anne leaves for college and says goodbye to her childhood friend, Diana—just like what I am doing.

"I kind of gathered something was wrong," she chokes. Our mules grow restless.

"You've been acting strange all evening." Her eyes sparkle with tears. "But you're doing the right thing—trusting in God. I will always be here for you, and I will miss you dearly."

"You know, I feel the same. I just found out not too long ago—you're the first friend I've told," I acknowledge, brushing a tear away.

"Ooh!" Diana exclaims in a nervous tone. "When are you planning on telling the Bricks?" she grinds her teeth in a nervous expression. She knows it will hit the group hard.

"I haven't even thought about it," I admit, wondering *how in the world* I will tell the class. "Honestly, I haven't even had time to process how this is changing my life permanently. I have no idea where I'm even going to live or go to school."

"When are you leaving?"

"It could be as far as next May," I say half-heartedly. I overheard Dad say we could leave as soon as this January or as far off as next May. But three months of childhood seems too short to comprehend, so I'm sticking to May.

"We must continue writing letters to each other," I persist, sounding like a nineteenth-century girl from a novel. Diana and I write letters every other week because neither of us likes to text.

"Oh, yes!" Diana agrees, and our faces light up. Worst case, we still have a whole semester together. Our conversation immediately shifts to the colleges we both want to attend and the distance between Oklahoma City and Ozark. Diana says she plans to attend an esteemed college in the Branson hills, and I express my desire to come back to Missouri for my lifelong dream university. College seems so wishful—it used to be a far-away fear of leaving home— but now it is *nothing* compared to the greater reality of moving to Oklahoma.

Time appears to have stopped while we sit on the mules, and so much has evolved over the course of a few simple words.

"We must make the most of this semester," Diana sits up in the saddle.

"Of course!" I agree, then add in a lower voice, "And don't say a word of this to anyone." Diana vows to do just that. "Want to gallop in the open field?" she asks again.

"Let's race!" I answer, kicking my heels and flying like a kite in the wind. Riding with your best friend in the sunset of the day is like medicine, healing, and therapeutic to an achy heart. Banjo and Apache race in unison. On the outside, it is as if nothing has changed; rather, our friendship is strengthened even further. The question still lingers whether our relationship will stand the test of time. Can anyone truly know?

When Diana drops me off at my house, I notice Annie and Papa's cars in the driveway, and I suspect it's already happened. I

77

walk past Bria, who's sobbing on the phone with her friend, and I see Angel twirling on a barstool at the countertop.

"What are you drawing?" I whisper, trying to be a connected older sister.

"Our home." Angel doesn't bother to look up from her crayon drawing.

"Why?"

"I don't want to forget it when we move," she replies in an even tone. Her words take my breath away. *Home.* Someday, where I am standing right now—my childhood cottage and all of its memories—will be someone else's house. The very thought sends a chill down my spine. I try to shake it off, but an unexpected sob from the living room sends me running down the hall.

Annie and Mom are hugging and crying, and Papa is shaking my dad's hand and saying words of encouragement. Papa has always been such a steadfast, encouraging man. I don't know how anyone can hold it together at a time like this. *But then again...look at Dad!* I think to myself. His face is relaxed and happy. I wish I were like that.

When Annie sees me standing behind Mom, she pulls away and squeezes me as if it's our last time to see each other. I'm all for dealing with emotions, but what I really need right now is time to think. I wear a numb front in order to survive this emotional room. So, once Annie releases me, I retreat down the hall into my dear, precious, newly-mine room. I just want to run away from the emotions at home, from friends and family members, and especially from anything related to Oklahoma.

Youth group finished late tonight. I am itching for a window to tell Jaclyn the news, but it almost seems impossible. Jaclyn leads the seventh-grade girls' small group and plays the guitar on the worship team, so it's not abnormal she's caught up in after-service obligations. I twirl her keys I've been holding onto since worship, as usual, so she doesn't forget about them in the youth room…that happened one night.

My eyes sparkle with premature tears as I think about how this is one of the few remaining nights we'll be out here together—sitting side by side in service, serving together on Sundays, experiencing missions' trips and camp memories and having deep talks by her car after service.

>Meet me by the basketball goal. I gotta talk to u.<

I send the text, though I doubt she'll check her phone before I see her. Ever since I was born, Wednesday nights have been blocked off for youth service and hanging out with cool teenagers. I practically grew up in a high school small group—making friends with teenagers as if they were my peers. Now it is strange to think that I am leaving the world of familiar church faces and even leaving my childhood awe of the teenage world. Tonight, especially, I feel so old and solemn. Like childhood is slowly disappearing.

As my mind begins to spiral into a black hole of fear, I fail to notice the shadow behind me.

"There you are," Jaclyn pops up behind me. "Sorry I'm late, the small group went long tonight, and I had to shut down the lights in the classroom."

"You're good," I smile, uneasy about the conversation we're about to have. We start to walk away from a growing crowd of rowdy junior high boys and stroll down a dark sidewalk. I throw Jaclyn her keys over her shoulder. She catches them one-handed and smiles at me. Our hair is frizzy from the humidity.

"How was your small group?" I stall as we come up on her silver car, Alfred.

"Pretty good," Jaclyn stares at her tennis shoes, walking one foot in front of the other. "I saw your text; did you want to talk about something?"

"Um, yeah," I stutter, stopping before we reach the end of the sidewalk. The parking lot lights beam down on our silhouettes. She patiently stops to listen, crossing her arms and tilting her head. *Maybe this isn't a good night,* I ponder, noticing her posture. Perhaps she has bucketloads of homework tonight. *Just call it off.* A thought sparks, but I quickly blow it out. I need to tell her right here, right now. I don't want her hearing it from someone else. I feel a lump in my throat as I begin to stutter the words that have haunted each conversation since yesterday.

"So…our family has been praying about something a lot," I begin, surprised to hear her mutter *"oh no"* under her breath. *Does she already know?*

"What?" I ask.

"I kind of wondered if this conversation was coming."

"Why?"

"Well, obviously something at camp," she adds in a scratchy, almost inaudible voice.

"Yeah," I admit, still unsure whether she knows what it is.

"So, what is it?" She avoids eye contact, waiting for me to finish. Her expression is somewhat annoyed, somewhat crushed.

"Jac, um, we've been praying about…moving…to…Oklahoma," I say once again, feeling like a parrot.

"Oh," she murmurs, eyes welling up with tears.

"I just found out not too long ago—it was totally unexpected. I mean, completely out of the blue. But then we heard these prophecies about our family doing something new, and suddenly Mom and Dad began to pray, and at camp, I had this vision of walking through this school hallway."

"Oh?"

"Get this, Jaclyn. I've never seen this school before in my entire life. It was such a vivid picture, and I couldn't get it out of my head. I still can't."

"So, you're going to a new school?"

"Eh, probably not," I shake off the chill. "We'll definitely be homeschooled in Oklahoma. Surely it's just a symbolic picture of change."

"Oh," she says again, confused.

"Anyways, before I could take the whole matter to court and petition against Mom and Dad's decision, I found ten moving boxes in front of my door, and I was told to keep the whole matter a secret until further notice. Well, now the news is out, so I wanted to tell you in person before you heard it from someone else," I explain the raw facts.

She lifts her glimmering brown eyes to mine and whispers the faint words: "When will you leave?"

"Probably January," I confess honestly, after hearing what Dad told Annie and Papa last night. Apparently, this thing is happening sooner than later.

Jaclyn brushes a tear away with her wrist.

"We still have over a dozen Wednesday nights we can spend together, so this isn't goodbye…" I reassure.

Jaclyn laughs. "We're going to have to make the most of this semester."

I turn around and see Dad's black Jeep waiting by the basketball goal. "Well, um, I gotta go."

"Okay," she gives me a long, bitterly sweet hug.

"I didn't mean for this to end so emotional," I say, and we both laugh to ease our tears away.

"Hey," she says slyly. "You still haven't done your podcast interview yet…"

"About that…" I stammer with a smile. "I thought surgery might've made me exempt?"

"You wish!" Jaclyn punches me in the arm.

We exchange one more hug before she walks toward Alfred, parked in its usual space since the day she received it for her sixteenth birthday. I watch her wipe her eyes in the rearview mirror before making a sharp turn out of the church parking lot.

My feet feel glued to the sidewalk. I can't seem to walk away. All I can feel is that my news of leaving is like a wedge between me and the rest of the world. Will this be the end of all of my friendships?

"Moment of Truth"

Summer left without saying goodbye. It's like I just looked up, and—*boom*—here I am, once again at school. Except this time, I'm walking into a new church building in the city of Springfield, just outside of Ozark. Due to the school drama that happened over the summer, our homeschool class now meets at a new co-op location. If I weren't so tied up in mouth surgery mishaps and moving, I would protest against this. But as I open the doors to this new building, I merely sigh and keep walking.

I never imagined I'd be so calloused. I've lived in the moment my whole life, caught up in the roar of the social world, and now it feels like I'm in another dimension. Like I am depressed or something. I pop a pain reliever in my mouth before walking into class. I need every ounce of energy I can muster before facing the Bricks.

"Spring Formal is going to be amazing this year!" Lexi, the one who keeps everyone in high spirits, exclaims at the lunch table. All of the Bricks are sitting alongside me and snacking on their signature lunches. I can literally predict what each girl brought just from my years of observation. Now everyone is looking at me like I'm supposed to carry on the ideas about the sophomore formal event, and while I'm normally happy to discuss coordinating dress colors and picking the restaurant, I'm just not in the mood. Still, I force a smile.

"What dress are you going to wear?" Ella turns to me.

"Ooh, what will you wear, Candice?" Catherine adds.

"I don't know yet," I laugh, rubbing my cheek (which has significantly decreased in size since my second surgery with my new doctor). Thinking on the spot, I add, "Maybe something blue and my hair up this year?"

"Ooh!" Two other Bricks grin, sharing a bag of seaweed chips.

"You always wear blue…" Lexi points out.

"But it looks very pretty on you," adds soft-spoken Grace, sipping her usual bowl of homemade chicken noodle soup.

"Thanks," I say numbly. They might think I'm offended; I'm really just half-present in the world right now.

Mrs. Hammond, our adored teacher, runs up to the lunch table. "Girls, I have really big news!"

I flinch. Kelly's eyes meet mine. *Did Mom tell her about the big news?*

"I just made a few calls to parents, and…*we are going to plan a trip to Europe this spring!*" she announces. *Whew. That was a close one.*

I slouch over my lunch plate. Everyone else shoots up from the benches.

"Oh, my word!"

"Are you serious?"

"This is going to be amazing!" They scream, giving hugs like it is Christmas morning. Once I gather what Mrs. Hammond said, I feel the excitement, too. But I feel so strange. I've heard from military kids like Catherine talk about how hard it is to change friend groups a dozen times, but I never thought I would experience it. *God, are you sure this is the right plan? Because I can't afford to alter the entire course of my life for a misunderstanding.*

"I'll share details after school," Mrs. Hammond smiles, patting the table like a drum then walking out of the lunchroom.

"Europe! Can you believe it?" Ella grabs my hand and grins.

"I really can't!" I mutter. I wonder if Mom would even let us go. *She wouldn't want us to miss a trip with the Bricks,* I reason. But what if we move in January? Then what?

Diana makes eye contact with me across the table. Her sad eyes make me want to scream. She has this look as if she's saying, *"I bet you can't go."* I know I'm being unrealistic expecting everyone to grieve when I grieve, but I really can't afford to burst into tears right now. It would totally blow my cover. I smile back at her to send the message, but she just shakes her head with a sorrowful look.

I'm so done with grieving.

It's the middle of September, and I still haven't had the nerve to tell Sophia about the *Big Move.* I haven't even texted her since school started. It's just too weird to think about. I mean, she's been one of my closest friends since I was barely old enough to *make* friends. And I know she's crazy busy with work, school, and cheer, but I've got to tell her at some point. I think it's best if I call her tonight and get it over with, but I'm really sick of riding this emotional rollercoaster over and over again. We've been in and out of family members' houses, exchanging tears and hugs like somebody died. It almost feels as if somebody did.

The more I think about this, the more I get worked up. It's been a few weeks since my second mouth surgery, and I'm on so many antibiotics I don't even feel like my real self. Maybe I'm experiencing an out-of-body compulsion. I've tried to distract myself with plans for my sixteenth birthday, but that just makes me sad to think it's my last time to have a birthday in Missouri.

Speaking of friends...I better soak up all of the nice feelings of having them right now. Because soon, I'm going to be friendless. Completely friendless.

Stop procrastinating, Candice. I slap my forehead. Sophia needs to know the truth, and she needs to hear it from me. I don't know how she's going to take it, but that's not something I can control. Breathe, Candice. Just do it.

>*Can I call u?*< I text, feeling guilty I haven't kept up small talk in what feels like forever.

>*Getting off work. Call in five:)*<

She responds, and I remember she works late on Thursdays. I pace the room, rehearsing my lines for what feels like an eternity, and then I hear my phone ring.

"Hey, girl!" she says in her usual cheerful manner. I hear her crank the keys in the background and the engine starting up. This is probably not the best time to drop such heavy news on her, but then again, when is it ever a good time to tell your best friend you're moving?

"Um…" I stutter. Here come the emotional tears. "First of all, I want to say I'm sorry for being such a poor friend the past few weeks. I've—we've—been going through a lot as a family, and I haven't been allowed to talk about it."

"I get it," she responds kindheartedly, and then I feel guilty for blaming it on family troubles. Sophia lost her brother in a car accident two years ago, and here I am, acting like this is some major crisis. I know I'm blowing it out of proportion, yet I don't know how to stop.

"Well, um…I don't really know how to say this…it's like the biggest thing that's ever happened to me," I say in between baby sobs. Sophia is silent on the other end. Who knows what she's thinking?

"No, I'm not pregnant," I laugh to ease the tension, knowing Sophia would holler. "And no, I'm not kicking you off of my bridesmaid list," I add. Now I realize it's time to cut the small talk and tell her the truth. *"I'm leaving Missouri and moving to Oklahoma."*

It's silent on the other end of the phone. I can't tell if she's mad, emotionless, or muted herself because she's crying. Well, here I am sobbing, so if she's not crying, the rest of this phone call is going to be extremely awkward.

Finally, I hear her voice break. *"No way,"* she says. Now I can hear her crying, which makes me cry even harder. I think the reason my stomach has been so sore is because I've been crying so much. And when I cry, it stirs up my mouth infection. Either way, it's a loss.

"Um, yeah," I say in between sniffles. We spend a good five minutes softly crying. "I just want you to know you've been the bestest, bestest friend, and I hope this doesn't change anything between us." I curl my legs to my chest and smile, thinking about all of our good times.

"I'm sure you're going to make a major impact on people's lives in Oklahoma. You're going to make new friends and have new opportunities, maybe even find a new hobby. I know it's sad, and I'm gonna miss you…so…much."

I marvel at how encouraging she is. But then again, it's Sophia. She's the very definition of encouraging. I wonder if I'll make friends like this in Oklahoma, but I highly doubt it.

The more I think about it, the more I consider finding a way out of this Oklahoma predicament. Maybe I *could* move in with my grandparents and visit my family on holidays…

Not a chance. *God, I'm going to obey you, even though my grief is unbearable.*

Ugh. Even as I'm trying—so desperately trying—to follow God and fully trust Him, today will be the *real* time I need to trust Him. I've held in the moving secret for several weeks at school, but Mom, Kelly, and I agree that it's time to tell the Bricks.

I'm usually trendy and original with my school outfits, but instead, I settle for jean shorts and a solemn black T-shirt. I feel like I should match my mood with my style: plain and gloomy. Before I walk out the door, I slip on my sneakers and look at myself in the mirror.

This is as good as it's gonna get, I sigh to myself, rubbing my swollen cheek. I then huff and puff my way out the door with an invisible raincloud over my head, ready for another amazing day of grieving.

I am getting used to "last times" in my life, but it doesn't make this one any easier. This is the final day I will walk in school, just like the rest of the Bricks; stable, carefree, and happily enjoying life in Missouri. Except I haven't *really* been enjoying this whole school year…unless you count sleeping in a skunk-smelling room covered in cardboard boxes fun. And to think that I'm about to separate myself from our high school sorority is both terrifying and depressing. I'm so sick of grief. I'm not sure how much more loss I can take. I'm dreading having to announce that we're moving and then carry on like normal for the rest of the semester. But waiting until the last minute to tell them would be cruel, so I don't have a choice, do I?

Kelly and I push open the double doors to school like we have a thousand times. My hands are shaking with nerves. I make a swift turn into the restroom for a brief second to check my face while Kelly continues walking to the classroom.

"I can't believe I'm about to say, 'We're moving,'" I mutter to Candice in the mirror after I make sure I am alone. It's as if moving is still a giant board game, and I am one of the players. But now that Kelly and I are verbalizing it to the masses, it is becoming a reality.

The bathroom door swings open, and Catherine walks past me.

"Morning, Candice!" she says cheerfully. For a split second, I ponder telling her in the bathroom. Maybe it would calm my nerves ahead of time before I announce it in front of the eleven sets of eyes. But then again, maybe it would prompt premature tears.

"Can you believe the news about Europe?" she yells from a stall.

Never mind, I'm not going to tell her right now and ruin her morning.

"And wouldn't it be absolutely amazing if we had our Spring Formal overseas?!" she continues. I haven't considered *that* possibility. What if we can't go to Europe? This means I won't ever have another Formal with the Bricks!

"Yeah, that would be amazing." I chuckle uneasily, shifting the weight of my backpack and walking out of the bathroom. "See you in class, Cat."

I shuffle my feet into the burnt-orange classroom like a lamb to slaughter and immediately lock eyes with Mrs. Hammond, who already knows from Mom about our announcement. I wonder when she wants us to tell everyone about the *Big Move*. Once everyone is seated and finishes their morning chit-chatting, Mrs. Hammond clears her throat in a commanding way.

"To begin today's class…Candice and Kelly Grace have something they would like to say."

I try my best not to laugh. I always have this sudden urge to laugh at the most inappropriate moments, like at my great-grandmother's funeral. I glance across the room at Kelly, who wears a look of resolve.

"You want me to start?" Kelly asks awkwardly. Of course, my emotions are rolling, and there's no turning around. I suck in tears and nod back.

"Well, you know how our dad preaches in different churches across the country?"

"Yeah," everyone unsurely acknowledges. The more Kelly avoids the news, the more I feel God nudge me to get to the main announcement.

I am inching forward in my chair, and words fumble out of my mouth. "This summer, God has been speaking to our family about change. At first, we didn't know what that change meant or how it would affect us, but I—we—asked God for clarity, and slowly but surely, things started to get specific. It was my Dad's decision, but he basically discerned what he felt God was telling us to do." I realize everything I said doesn't make sense since I failed to mention the prophecies, but before I can add to my words, Kelly speaks up.

"We've never moved before," Kelly blurts out. "But we will hopefully still be in Missouri to finish the school year. We are… moving to Oklahoma."

It's an eerie sort of silence. I look down at my shoes while the words sink in.

"But we can always come back for Bible studies, parties, and formal, of course," Kelly adds, though it's plain it will be impossible to still be a part of the class. As I search the faces around me, my face turns to stone. Murmured sobs trickle through the classroom.

"That was it," Mrs. Hammond says with a smile. *"That was it?" Are you serious?* But now that I think about it, she couldn't have said it better.

That *was* it. The greatest *it* to ever impact Candice Gibbons' life.

"Let's pray for Candice and Kelly as their family experiences such a tremendous change. It is also so cool that God has called your family through transition," Mrs. Hammond guides the atmosphere.

My tears are partly sensational. Though I've cried a dozen times in the past month, *true* tears have not formed and probably will not until my first night in Oklahoma City.

"Let's circle around the girls and pray." Everyone stands up like robots. Arms enclose me into another Bricks prayer circle. It feels like another Bible study, not a monumental farewell ceremony. And even though I know this isn't truly "goodbye," I am rattled at the heavy, invisible cloud that seems to loom over our circle.

"I'll pray," Lexi speaks up. "Heavenly Father, thank you for these wonderful girls…"

Her prayer stops like a record screech.

"Hold on, guys," she stops, to which everyone lifts their heads. "We need to pray like a Bible study prayer. I want to hear all of you."

This sends a chuckle throughout the circle. I smile at Lexi.

"Thank you, God, for Candice and Kelly."

"Give them strength as they leave their friends."

"Let them remember this is Your will, God."

"Go before them, God…" Whispers fill the room, followed by tears. The vision of walking down unfamiliar hallway replays in my mind. I'm scared to think that actually might come true. But I bet it's just a visual of uncomfortable change that is coming, not like I'm actually going to go to a real school.

As Lexi wraps up the prayer, sobs are shared in every direction. I hug everyone in the room, but I can't tell exactly who they are. My eyes are too blurry. Suddenly, everyone starts overpromising things to lighten the mood.

"Hey, you guys can drive back up to school every week!"

"We'll facetime you at every Bible study!"

But as encouraging as these remarks make me feel, I warn myself not to let them sink in. I mean, we've all been there: making hasty promises in a moment of emotion. I thank them, and then everyone eventually settles with the news, so the day passes on in a disturbingly average way.

I focus myself on an intricately detailed drawing of our house through every subject, so when I move away, I won't forget what it looks like. And then I rip the page out of my composition journal and throw it in the trash can as if it was silly to draw a picture of the only house I've ever known. I think they call this living in a state of denial.

But seriously, how can anyone concentrate on school when their life is falling apart?

"Three…two…one, and you're live!" Kurt gives a thumbs up from the sound booth.

"Welcome, students, back to another youth podcast! Today we are interviewing our very own youth podcast host, Candice Gibbons, who's going to be sharing what's been happening in her life," says my youth pastor.

I cringe at his words, searching for some mediocre topics to discuss, like what I ate for breakfast. I've put off this interview long enough, given all of my surgery complications. Now, it's go-time.

"Why don't you start off by telling us a little bit about yourself?" he asks, turning toward me. The auditorium room is empty, thankfully, with the exception of Jaclyn in the front row and a student named Kurt in the sound booth.

"I am the oldest of six, a pastor's kid here at church. My dad speaks at churches all over the country, though, and I love the outdoors. I am homeschooled, and I think that's pretty cool. Oh, and I lead these podcasts every week," I add. That had to be the worst bio I've ever given about myself, but I don't really care. It's not as if these people are going to see me for much longer. I'll have to rethink what I say to people when I move to Oklahoma…

"Wow, being the oldest of six must be stressful!" he acknowledges with a chuckle. "So, Candice, you and your family are leaving Missouri and moving to Oklahoma City! How exciting! Walk me through the emotions that you've had through this process. What will you miss the most?"

"Miss…the most?" I repeat slowly, gripping my handheld microphone and begging for help from Jaclyn. She nods sympathetically, silently telling me I've got this. *God, please help me say the right thing.* I pray.

Everyone's staring at me with expectation, and Honest Candice can't just plop out a church-y answer, like *"Trust in the Lord with all of your heart"* unless she truly believes it. Candice is such a down-to-earth person she might totally spit out, *"I hate Oklahoma, and I'm not sure I trust God with this whole crisis right now!"* before processing her words. *Uh oh, here it comes…*

"Honestly, I was shocked," I blurt out. "I mean, I thought I would live in Missouri my whole life. I saw the word 'freedom' written on this year's summer, so it was hard to believe I was being called to do something beyond my agenda. It's so hard to leave all of my family, friends, school, and church. If any of you students listening have ever moved, you know what it's like." An awkward pause follows.

"Wow, ugh…I can't imagine." My youth pastor shakes his head.

Get me out of this room! Tears flood inside of me. I vaguely see Jaclyn lift her hand and signal me to keep talking.

"But you know what?" I struggle to continue. "I'm…I'm excited to see what God has for me in Oklahoma." My throat chokes out the words. "I know God can use me there to reach people. Besides, I've given my whole life to Him. I've chosen to trust God, and it's not easy. But when I do, I feel at peace—you know, like everything's going to be alright. That's what I can bank on."

Just by saying these words publicly, it feels as if a weight has dropped off my chest. Jaclyn smiles at me. I shift in my chair and smile back. God is giving me such a subtle peace about the future. "Yeah. I trust Him with everything," I end.

"Accepted"

Towering trees of orange and yellow fold high above my head like a tunnel of gold flowers. The sun beams down on me like a flashlight through the tree leaves, creating kaleidoscope designs on my blue raincoat. My brown leather boots crunch over the fallen twigs and acorns covering the blueish asphalt road. I twirl Charlie's leash around my hand and tilt my head toward the sky. Picture-perfect cottages stretch far upon rolling terrain, sheltered by evergreens, oaks, and maples. I squint my eyes and study each tree, hoping I won't forget this nostalgic neighborhood path.

The fourth week of October is arriving swiftly. Two more weeks and I'll be sixteen. This is my last autumn to walk this trail of my childhood. Oh, how I've taken for granted my cottage neighborhood hidden in a hilly forest! You never realize what you have until it's gone. Why have I considered it normal to walk my neighborhood like it is a hospital hallway, blind to its beauty? I've missed so much! Thank goodness I see the splendor of it now, or else I would never have realized what I left behind. I know I joke about Missouri being the best place ever, and you probably think I'm biased, but I daresay I would praise it even if I wasn't a native. (See it for yourself—especially in the fall.)

Now that October has begun, I am more than ready to enjoy all of my fall traditions: going to the local craft fair with Diana, riding horses at Riverview Ranch, sipping chai lattes, and playing in the leaves with the girls. Of course, this fall will already be different without The Great Oak's leaves in the yard.

Nevertheless, fall is such a breath of fresh air from the pressures of moving. Yesterday, I broke out my box of fall sweaters and tied on my brown boots to play on the farm with my cousins. I am planning on going to the Farmer's Market with Diana and lending a hand with Poppy's pumpkin patch at the farm on the weekends.

Forget Alabama. Forget mouth surgery. Forget Oklahoma.

Goodbye, Missouri fall.

It isn't long before I find myself squished in the back of our family GMC...driving to Oklahoma.

"We have to buy a lot so we can build a house there," Mom tells us in the car.

"But...this week? Why can't we wait until January? What about the craft fair? And my birthday! Fall is my favorite season..."

"Don't worry, Candice. Oklahoma has a fall season too," Mom laughs.

"Not the same," I mutter. "When I went to camp there this summer, the mud was red, mom. *Red!*"

Mom laughs. I gape at her incredulously.

"Don't worry. We'll be back in time for your big sixteenth birthday," Dad assures me. Still, I sink lower in my chair and pout on the way to Oklahoma. I tried to convince Mom to let me stay with grandparents so I could enjoy my final fall in the Ozarks, but she didn't buy it.

"Wouldn't it be great if we built a cottage in Oklahoma City just like we have here?" she beams.

"Uh-huh," I sigh, turning to the window. I'm all for bringing a piece of Missouri to Oklahoma, but I'm not liking how fast everything's happening. The further we are from Missouri and the closer we inch to Oklahoma, the fall colors slowly and subtly disappear.

Oh, no. Mom and Dad are talking about sending Kelly and me to a *real* school.

"Pastor Jackson's kids go there," Dad whispers, turning onto the interstate.

"Isn't it close to the lots we're looking at?" Mom doesn't know I'm listening.

"Very close."

Little Candice might actually go to a real school?!

But I don't need a new school! I think, unzipping my suitcase at the hotel we're staying in for two weeks. *I'm in school with the best class ever. I can't imagine going anywhere else!*

Wait a minute. Maybe this is the reason God's moving me to Oklahoma. I *did* have a vision at camp about being at a school—something tied to the word "sacrifice." As much as I hate to say it, the puzzle pieces are fitting together.

"What does 'OEH' stand for?" I stare in disbelief at the proud letters on the red and white school sign.

"Oklahoma Excellence High school," Kelly answers.

"Well, if that's not a high society name—" I start to say, but Mom interrupts me.

"I'm sure it is a great Christian school, Candice. You remember meeting Pastor Jackson at New Life Church?"

"And?"

"His son, Kevin Jackson, is a freshman here. And you know how much we love and respect their family." *AKA the whole reason we're moving here is because of their family*, I think to myself.

"And no, they don't wear uniforms," Mom adds, reading my face. She knows exactly what I'm imagining: rows of well-off, A+

high schoolers dressed in plaid skirts and knee socks marching down blinding fluorescent halls.

When we walk into the school, I don't really pause to think about what's going on. *This is not my school, and it never will be because I already go to school in Missouri.* I reason illogically, as if I'm staying with the Bricks forever. Thankfully, the students are all in classes, so I'm not feeling too self-conscious in my plaid shirt and Dutch braids to think about running into any of them.

I still can't grasp the fact that we are actually moving to Oklahoma. And considering how Little Candice is handling this crisis so far, there are plenty of reasons to be concerned about how I'm going to react when I do move into a new house. At least I have the "trusting God" part down.

I glance up from the checkered floors and hear the admissions counselor talking about all of the school's academic success. I decide to innocently wander off down a hallway and explore the place for myself. After all, I need to know what I'm getting myself into.

You've got to be kidding me.

I turn a corner and see a hallway that looks just like the one in my vision at camp. Except, of course, no students are in it...yet.

The ceiling is low and white, just like my vision.

Red lockers and black and white checkered floors line the halls, just like the vision.

I am standing on the far end with my head held high, just as I pictured.

Every school probably has a hall like this. I reason, shaking off the chills. Since I've been homeschooled my whole life, I only have so many images of what a "real" school is like. Technically, my only interpretations are the schools I've seen in movies. It can't be *that* far off.

Returning to our tour, I stare up at the high ceiling with sky windows. It makes our voices echo. And since the rest of the school is so eerily quiet, I feel like every single classroom is listening to my mom explain our life story, including how my math grades are below average.

"I couldn't survive here," I whisper to Kelly, who, unlike me, is an excellent academic student. To me, grades are overrated, and abstract creativity is far too often overlooked. But part of me likes the idea of having a challenge. This looks exactly like a movie set. I've always wanted to see what it would be like to go to a real high school!

The tour ends in less than thirty minutes, and I am glad when it does. The whole building was cold and smelled like hand sanitizer—like a hospital.

"We will get in touch with you when we find out when we're moving into our rental house," I hear Mom say.

You've got to understand I've never been to an actual school. I caught a glimpse of public school just to ride the bus, eat cafeteria food, and experience what I saw in movies for a few weeks when I was in elementary school, but this is different. These aren't fourth graders I'll be dealing with; we're talking private-schooled high school kids. The stakes are astronomically high.

I'm sure public-schooled kids would quickly tell me real high school isn't like what's played on TV, but who am I to know? I've never had my own locker, changed classes at the bell, switched buildings for lunch, or joined a school sport, let alone seen a principal's office. It all sounds so fantastical. Maybe this is my chance to see what it's like!

After sightseeing one empty lot after another, Mom and Dad finally found one to fit their liking. To my relief, it's a little outside of the city, though you can still hear the interstate from my bedroom. Dad found a rental house, too, somewhere close to OEH. But I'm not really worried about what that looks like. After all, Dad said our new house should be finished by the time school gets out in May, so we shouldn't have to live there very long.

Thankfully, now I am back in Missouri, and my birthday is on its way. I am determined to shove anything related to our life in

Oklahoma until after Christmas. As Jaclyn says, I need to live in the moment.

After a brisk walk with Charlie in the neighborhood, I snag a gingerbread cookie off the counter and head toward my room. The house is quiet and empty, which is rare when you live with five kids and a chihuahua-yorkie mix puppy dog. At least I was able to enjoy having my own space for a few months...because, come January, Kelly and I will be sharing a room in the rental house.

I quickly open my bedroom door to see Mom and Kelly sitting on my bed. I guess it doesn't matter whether you have your own room or not; there's really no such thing as personal privacy in a family of eight.

"There she is!" Kelly exclaims.

"Why didn't you knock?" Mom asks, hiding papers behind her back.

"I don't find it customary to knock on *my* bedroom door," I say, picking up dirty laundry that's scattered around my room for a few days now. I'm usually a clean person, but hey, I used to think I would be a Missouri resident for life. Things can change.

To my relief, Mom doesn't say anything about the laundry.

"Well...we have exciting news!" Mom pulls out the papers from behind her back. "Since it's official, we are moving right after Christmas, I thought we should get the ball rolling."

"Okay?" I walk into the bathroom and brush my hair out of habit.

"I just got off a call with Mrs. Gray, Oklahoma Excellence's admissions counselor, and she says you both need to fill out these forms concerning your previous education and grades so you can apply for the next school semester!" Mom beams, holding the papers in the air.

"Isn't that exciting?" Kelly squeals, covering her mouth.

"Woah, woah, woah..." I drag out. "I don't want to even think about Oklahoma until January. Can this wait?" I plug my ears.

"Can this wait?" Mom repeats with exasperation. "No, this can't wait! Do you think I *want* to be packing up my home and family moving to this...this...city? Candice, life's not about what we want.

I'm over here trying to plan your future education so you can get into the college of your dreams. The least you can do is cooperate," she says firmly.

My knees start to shake, and I crumble to the floor. "I'm sorry. I know you're under a lot of pressure. It's just, I don't know if I want to go there. Plus, I may not even get accepted because of my math grades." I curl up into a ball.

"Oh, stop exaggerating. When they read your writing, you will blow them away!" Kelly overly encourages, as usual, pushing the pen and paper towards me.

"And I know you try your best," Mom says in a more sympathetic tone. Maybe seeing her fifteen-turning-sixteen-year-old daughter curled up in a ball triggers a twinge of guilt in Mom.

"It's embarrassing," I point out the obvious. "They might have to put me in the junior high math program!"

"What could it hurt to apply?" Mom answers, and Kelly smiles at her words. I gather they both realize how extreme my mind is reacting. I know I sound extreme too, but my emotions are swirling around like an erupting volcano, and I'm about to explode with tears.

But despite all my efforts, I find myself reluctantly filling out the papers and writing down my measly GPA. I can't believe I'm signing my life to an Oklahoma institution. *God, I'm not ready for this.*

The answer arrived faster than any of us expected. During break at school on Monday, Kelly and I simultaneously received an email notification, and all the Bricks gathered around to see what the fuss was about.

"*No way!*" Kelly whispered in disbelief.

"What?" I asked, still fumbling for my phone in the bottom of my backpack.

"I…we just got accepted into OEH!" she announced.

A wave of fear swept over me. *This is really happening!* And there we were with the Bricks—one of the most awkward places to announce our school acceptance, right in front of the closest people who we're leaving behind. I could only imagine what *they* were thinking about all of this. Looking for an escape from all the puzzled faces around me, I studied the email and reread every word.

We are excited to announce the acceptance of Candice M. Gibbons to Oklahoma Excellence High School's Sophomore Class. Please review the handbook and email Mrs. Gray sent with any questions you may have.
Go Eagles!

I smiled at my name tied to the word *acceptance*. Maybe this would be a launching pad for my new life. Maybe God *was* going to allow me to thrive at OEH. I started to believe God's call on my life to move was all going to work out now that I had a landing place. I pictured myself walking in wearing a perfect outfit with my hair blowing in the wind, everyone clapping as I strode through the door.

A hand rubbed my back.

"I'm so excited for you, Candice!" Diana sincerely congratulated. I was quickly snapped out of my trance and felt a wave of guilt rush over me. I didn't know how to respond. What was I supposed to say?

"Thank you, friend." I smiled back. Should I have shown my inner excitement, or would it appear that I was excited about leaving the class? I couldn't decide which emotions to show, so I gulped back a sentimental choke and gave her a hug. A few other Bricks joined in the celebration. Even Mrs. Hammond congratulated us. My heart was full of such earnest emotions tied to both Missouri and Oklahoma; I didn't know how to act.

Everything was changing too fast.

"The Last Birthday"

It is 6 a.m. I roll out of my trundle bed and plug in the Christmas lights hanging around my window. The sky is dark and clear. The moon is bright and full. I run my fingers through my thick, messy hair and breathe deep. I'm officially a sixteen-year-old!

Eager to start the age off right, I decide to throw on my work-out clothes and slip out for a run. The air is cold and misty, just like a classic October morning. Dark fog hovers over crisp trees. I run laps on the driveway because the late autumn sunrise makes it too dark for a full neighborhood run. Immediately, the humidity out-side makes me sweat, but I don't stop. Running is becoming a cop-ing mechanism. Today, especially, something drives me to run with urgency—like I am running from something. Maybe I am subcon-sciously running from Oklahoma, or maybe I am running towards childhood nostalgia.

As I huff and puff my way inside, the smell of bacon and eggs catches my attention. I suspect hot cinnamon rolls are in the oven, and I hear Mom humming and clanking pots and pans in the kitchen.

"What are you doing!" she yells in a whisper.

"Oh, sorry! I forgot the birthday tradition that you're not sup-posed to come out of your room until called," I say with all honesty, untying my tennis shoes and tiptoeing back to my room. *"You never saw me..."* I whisper down the hall.

In the Gibbons family, birthdays mean a buffet-style break-fast complete with juice, eggs, bacon, fruit, and cinnamon rolls.

Additionally, Mom breaks out leftover birthday streamers from the last family party and adorns the kitchen with decorations. And since this is my sixteenth—a big one—I expect nothing less.

But sixteen is already starting off on the wrong side.

I stare at my slightly less swollen face in the bathroom mirror. The surgery inflammation hasn't worn off completely, and picture day didn't go so well last week. Still, despite my swollen cheeks, I am determined to celebrate with my friends and family and enjoy my last birthday in our house as normally as possible. I've already decided to be thankful even though I know I'm not getting a car since Dad and Mom are clear that I'd have to work for my own vehicle. Besides, the best part about birthdays is spending them with friends and family.

"You can come out now!" Jordan shouts, running into my room. It's time to face the family. *Don't let your emotions get in the way. Don't let your emotions get in the way.* I repeat to myself.

I walk into the kitchen, and everyone says "surprise!" and blows party horns. I hear the old sixties song *Sweet Sixteen* playing on the kitchen speaker.

After breakfast, everyone steps into the living room for presents. I can tell each person's mind is fixed on moving details, but they are trying to be merry for my sake. Mom and Dad tell me to close my eyes while they fumble around with a large object covered by a blanket. And while I'm not totally convinced on the whole "earn your own car" propaganda, I don't know why they're telling me to close my eyes. Wouldn't they take me outside if it was a car?

"You can open now!" they say.

It's definitely not a car.

I open my eyes and see a bronze-stained *cello* sitting upright in a black stand. I've always thought the cello was such a beautiful instrument, but this is definitely a surprise.

"Wow, um…Thank you!" I exclaim, plucking the strings with my fingers. The wood is a shiny, fiery orange and unusually slender, in contrast to most cellos that are dark brown and rather plump. The strings are deeper and calmer than the violin I played as a child.

"We'll get you lessons in Oklahoma," Mom says quickly.

Oh, I get it. This is supposed to make the move easier on me. Nice try, Mom.

"Oklahoma, here we come!" Mom says cheerily, and immediately everyone groans.

"Remember why we're moving there," Dad reminds us. "God called us to go."

"I am excited," I say, mostly to convince myself to be a Meg. I pick up the bow lying beside the cello and position my fingers in what I think looks like the right place.

"Why don't you play something?" Kelly suggests. I've only played the cello once when Mom rented one while I was recovering from foot surgery in eighth grade. I lean the cello on my chest and softly strum all four strings. There is something so sad and mournful about a cello; its lowest strings seem to be crying. I draw in a deep breath and try to think of an easy song I can find on the cello. Lifting the bow to the strings, I close my eyes and let my fingers do the work.

"I love *All in All*," Mom says, smiling at the music. The hymn sounds especially grand, echoing throughout the living room ceiling. My fingers push intensely on the strings and I tighten my brow. Once everyone realizes what hymn it is, their voices echo into the arched ceiling. The lyrics sing:

> *You are my strength when I am weak.*
> *You are the treasure that I seek.*
> *You are my All in All.*

And if there is ever a time our family needs His strength, it is now. Ending the song with a dramatic finish, I open my eyes to see everyone solemnly looking at the ground. Heavy silence rests in the room. We all know it is only a matter of moments before it is time to say goodbye to the house. This moment is a special reminder of how much we're going to need each other. Moving is going to be hard, but we are still going to have seven familiar faces around the dinner table every night.

Our family is about to go through our greatest trial yet.

Don't tell me I am being dramatic. Tonight is literally the last time I will see most of my Missouri friends, and so I decided to wear a black, lacy dress to symbolize my deep feelings of loss. My hair is curly and highlighted—Mom let me get my hair highlighted for the first time!—and Sophia endured the two boring hours of watching me in the hairstylist chair–she is the best.

On a sad note, Mom said this is the last night I can wear this dress…apparently, it's too short. But despite feeling a little scandalous in this dress, I am full of joy. Nearly everyone who I invited is able to come—even people who might have deep-seated issues with me have come out of respect. Moving has its perks. It's kind of like a funeral—you get to see who truly cares about you. Except, unlike a funeral, you're alive to enjoy it.

Jazz music softly hums in the background. Twig trees adorned in fairy lights scatter the venue. Before dinner is served, Poppy leads a special birthday prayer over the night, and Papa snaps pictures of everyone in the photobooth Kelly happily arranged. We feast on trays of breadsticks and pasta, drink sparkling ciders, and then munch from a dessert table decorated with tiny delicacies like cheesecake squares and macaroons.

The Bricks are busily chatting away with one another, and Diana, along with my former dance team friends from eighth grade, have seated themselves in a corner to converse all things dance. Angel and Jordan are running back and forth from the dessert table, and while some of my friends are affectionately watching a slideshow of my childhood on a projector screen, I hug friend after friend who I haven't seen for years.

Sophia reminds me it's our eighth birthday party to spend together. "You know I've come to your birthdays since your nine-year-old carnival party," she says, biting into a breadstick.

"You better come down to Oklahoma for my seventeenth," I warn back.

She laughs but doesn't agree. This is where I realize how my friends can't arrange their lives around mine once I move. Sophia is moving off to college next fall. I am learning to accept how our relationship may change.

After dinner, Mom passes out a quiz on who knows Candice best. As both of my grandmas fervently compete for the title, I watch my friends ask each other questions and write in answers. Nevertheless, it is my dear friend Abby from church who surpasses even my family members!

"Time for karaoke!" Mom announces, and everyone gathers around for the challenge of all challenges (Sophia and I win). To wrap up the festivities, Catherine and I lead the Bricks signature dance called the "Farm Animal Dance"—created in one of those weird moments on a late-night road trip. I can't believe the participation rate. Everyone—including my most reserved friends, siblings, and cousins—joins in the dance circle. A bond of unity if I've ever seen one.

I start to tear up over some particularly meaningful presents and earnestly thank people for all of my gifts. Each one was heartfelt and attached to a card of deepest friendship. I couldn't be more grateful.

When it's time to sing happy birthday, the candle formation spelling out "Happy 16" catches on fire, and everyone sings at an incredible speed. The room shakes with laughter as I earnestly blow out the flames before it engulfs the strawberry cake altogether. Before everyone leaves, I hand each party guest a heartfelt letter, expressing my thankfulness for our friendship.

Feeling full of gratitude, I sit at an empty table and thank God for sixteen years of blessed friendships: sixteen years of parties, sleepovers, camps, playdates, and sisterly bonding. I could sit here all night and contemplate my wonderful life.

But there's work to be done. Gathering the remains of the pasta, I help Dad load his black Jeep and thank him for staying at the party, even with his back pain.

"I wouldn't miss it for the world," he says, organizing my presents in the back seat. "You must feel so special to have so many people care about you."

"It was worth it," I respond. "I'm glad I spent most of my life investing in relationships. Friends really do make life better."

"And relationships are the only thing you can take to heaven," he reminds me, shutting the trunk.

"I know. I was surprised to see some of the faces that showed up tonight. Others I think of and smile because they're girls that wouldn't be living for God without the influence of godly voices."

"Like yours," Mom says, bringing out the last of the presents.

"You are such a light to your friends," Dad looks me in the eyes. I return the smile as my arms quiver with goosebumps.

What if it's not like this in Oklahoma?

My mind is immediately transferred to the halls OEH, nervously walking by myself.

"I hope it will be that way in Oklahoma," I throw out, walking towards the doors to the empty party room.

"If you're walking with God, everything will work out," Dad assures me.

As my birthday streamers are shoved into cardboard boxes, I think about the blessings I've overlooked in my day-to-day life. My friends are trustworthy and godly. My parents are loving and supportive. My grandparents are welcoming and interested in my life. I have friends just about everywhere I go.

God, please help me make new friends in Oklahoma, I pray. Relationships take time, and it all depends on the kind of people you are surrounded with in your daily life. So, if I am determined to make new friends in Oklahoma, I have to be a good friend myself, and since I can't be a good friend *and* an emotional wreck, I should start pulling it together.

"A Grieving Dilemma"

A frosty sadness settles on the land. The cows are no longer mooing in the pasture behind our house, and the branches on our oak trees are bare. All of the leaves have fallen and died. It reminds me of how empty our house will be in less than two months.

October is over, and I didn't even get a chance to go to the craft fair because of all of the busyness. Mom has been preoccupied packing boxes, and that means Kelly and I are the chefs and babysitters of the house. To add to our disunity, Dad is completely slammed trying to finish his trips of the year as well as renovating parts of the house—a list that continues to grow—and the rest of my siblings are hopping from one friend's house to another saying their goodbyes.

I haven't seen Sophia since my birthday party, but I plan to go with her to Silver Dollar City one more time when the park is decorated in Christmas lights. She offered to help me pack, but I don't think that would be a good idea, seeing as though we'd have to face my childhood pictures and keepsakes of us over the years. I would be an emotional wreck.

Jaclyn and I dressed up as bank robbers and won third place in the church costume competition on October 31st. We had lots of fun getting ready at her house—stuffing pillowcases with trash bags to make money sacks, untangling each other's masks, and snapping pictures in our matching striped shirts. I can't believe that was our last harvest celebration together.

Diana and I have been soaking up every class we share together and have continued to send letters back and forth about the move, which has truly helped me process everything. Her heart of loyalty reassures me that she will be just a phone call away, just the simple press of a button away from hearing her familiar voice.

Still, other people aren't aiding the situation. One girl keeps telling me everything's going to be okay—like every other well-meaning person on the planet—but even she knows that everything's not okay. *Nothing's* okay.

My room feels like an empty hospital room—with my white bed frame and bleak walls—but my heart is set on keeping out my mini blue Christmas tree until the very last second. No matter what the rest of the house looks like, Christmas will not be shoved in *my* moving boxes.

It's been cloudy all weekend. I've cried so much about moving. What scares me most is knowing "deep Candice" hasn't kicked in yet. The only Candice that's here is emotionally sentimental Candice in a short-term I'm-having-an-emotional-day-but-tomorrow-will-be-better Candice. But despite my grief, I am still all in with this. I am not second-guessing God nor second-guessing myself. Oklahoma is exactly where God wants me to be, so it is the safest place I can position myself.

Isn't it obvious? I'm on a teeter-totter of emotions. One day I am hyped up about OEH, and the next minute I am lying on the carpet crying about how many years I've walked on it. Call me crazy, but anyone who's ever moved before knows exactly what it's like.

I am still in shock after Dad announced at the dinner table last night that during the two weeks leading up to Christmas, we will be in Oklahoma moving half of our stuff into the rental house, and Kelly and I will be shadowing students at OEH. I literally just prayed to God that I could enjoy Thanksgiving and Christmas without anything tied to the word *Oklahoma* interfering. I don't know if I'm more upset about moving over my belongings and they'll never come back to Missouri or that the joy of Christmas is going to be completely dampened. When will we decorate cookies or go caroling with friends if we're in Oklahoma most of the month? Never, that's when.

*   *   *

"I just don't know if I'm going to fit in. Here I am, a homeschooled PK, and I have no experience whatsoever at a private school. How do they even know where their classes are? Like, don't all school hallways look the same?" I say to Gigi after supper, holding my mug of hot apple cider. It is our traditional Thanksgiving dinner at the farm, and sure enough, everyone's in and out of conversations concerning Oklahoma. It is inescapable.

Gigi rubs my hand and sighs. She is my constant confidant.

"Oh, you'll figure it out in no time, honey. And there will be some stuck-up girls there, but you are so beautiful they'll be trying to be friends with you!" she assures me, a choke rising in her throat. I feel guilty for talking about moving when that is the reason everyone is so somber tonight, but it does help to process it aloud.

"What if I run track?" I change the subject, knowing she would have a fit over me joining a sport...especially because I'm not the athletic type like most of my cousins. The idea hits me out of nowhere.

Gigi chokes on her apple cider. "Why would you sign up to kill yourself? You know your feet are too delicate after having surgery and screws put in."

"I know, but I've always enjoyed running. Remember how the doctor said there's nothing else I can do but enjoy life as much as I can? And since I had to stop dancing for good, I've missed having an activity." I look down at the abnormal shape of my feet outlined in my fluffy Christmas candy cane socks.

"Why don't you be a cheerleader or something else pretty? Track is a sport that makes you all sweaty and red-faced," Gigi scrunches up her nose. "You don't want *that*."

I laugh and shake my head. "Cheerleaders are cliquish, at least in the movies. Picture all of that makeup and hairspray and mini skirt madness involved in being the perfect cheerleader. Running, on the other hand, is so freeing! I like to sweat; it's like this high comes over you. Plus, running with a team would help me make friends," I add.

"You'll tell the coach you have foot problems; you hear?" she leans forward with a look of disapproval.

"I'll mention it when I shadow a student in December," I agree. But honestly, I don't even know if I want to join track. Everyone, including me, knows it's a crazy idea.

Gigi switches the conversation to my Christmas wish list, which isn't too entertaining this year. But, as always, spending one-on-one time with Gigi shifts me into a calm and content state of mind.

"It's like you're breaking up the family," I hear a relative tell Dad as the men watch football. It still seems no one seems to fully understand the seriousness of God's mission for us in Oklahoma.

"Oklahoma...of all the places!" an uncle throws out over dinner. "What's the congregation like at New Life?" The table is filled with tantalizing dishes of southern cooking: fried chicken, smoked ham and turkey, homemade mashed potatoes, black-eyed peas, green beans, deviled eggs, homemade rolls, fruit salad, and a dessert table in the corner with ooey-gooey butter cake, chocolate brownies, pound cake, and sugared strawberries.

I bite my lip and wait for Dad's response. He is always calm and collected, never judgmental or snappy, though he is direct in his answer.

"New Life Church is mostly African American," he states.

"Y'all are going to stick out like sore thumbs!" another relative chimes in, laughing at Dad's comment.

I have never really thought about the cultural side until this moment. Ozark is ninety percent white, so I don't even have a reference point for the culture shock I'm about to witness.

Things are about to get interesting.

I'm so done having to sympathize with other people who are struggling over our move to Oklahoma. One minute they're grieving, and I'm pulled together for the moment, and the next minute I am feeling sentimental about leaving Ozark; it seems like everyone is waving us out of town. I know it sounds insensitive, but I only have so many tears to cry. For example, a few minutes ago, my preteen sisters, Bria and Allison, stood angrily in my room.

"Listen to what Bria's friend just told her…" Allison demanded.

"What exactly did this *friend* say about our family?" I interrogated, searching their faces.

"She said that we are so selfish, and we need to realize that we're not the ones who have it hard. She said our family gets it "easy" because we get a new house." Bria's eyes burned with fury.

"Can you believe the nerve of that girl?" Allison said, playing with her ballerina necklace.

"She's just grieving like all of us," said Kelly understandingly, opening the door to the bathroom while she brushed her hair.

"Yeah, the problem is, she has no idea how hard this is on us," Bria spoke my thoughts.

"And we don't know how hard it is on other people," Kelly added, smoothing her silky hair.

"It's true," I admitted through gritted teeth. "We need to learn to be sensitive to other people and not so consumed with our emotions."

Still, I know how hard it is to implement my advice. Just yesterday afternoon, Annie walked into my room and silently stared at me for a good twenty seconds.

"Hi!" I said cheerfully, glancing up from my homework.

Annie let out a dramatic huff, remaining frozen in the doorway.

"Is…something wrong?" I asked.

Her eyes searched the room as if she was seeing it for the last time.

"Someday, I'm going to walk in, and you won't be in your room. Someday, you'll be far gone, and I'll never get to see you in little moments like this."

A huge knot formed in my throat. "You know I don't want to leave you."

"And yet…here you go!" she said, like it was my choice. I shook my head with a sorrowful face, as if to say I can't help that God is doing this. Annie extended her arms and walked toward me, reading the pain in my eyes.

"I wish I could stay in Missouri," I said, burying my face in her chest.

Her squeeze was grippingly tight. "We'll always be here for you," she said, releasing the hug.

And with that, she walked out of the room, closing the door behind her. My heart longed to tell her about my inward grief—how I really wouldn't be doing this if God hadn't called me—but I was at a loss for words. If only the world could read my journal, then maybe everyone would understand how I'm trying so desperately hard to hold it together.

The winter chill rushes through my vent and blows the pages of my journal. The sky is bleak, cloudy, and gray, but knowing Missouri, there won't be any snow until January. I'm wearing my fluffy brown house shoes and my rubber ducky bathrobe over my clothes, attempting to stay warm. Our heat stopped working last night. The stove broke while cooking Mom's new try at chicken casserole, so Mom and Dad are at the appliance store in search of a new stove (I set up a movie for the kids so I could spend a few minutes writing). I'm starting to wish Mom had picked a prayer for confirmation besides "let everything fall apart." But today seems normal enough. For some reason, I have good handwriting today, and all of my cursive "F's" and "L's" are quite satisfying.

As I conclude today's journal entry with a contented smile, someone knocks on the door.

"May I enter?" Kelly asks in her sweet, feminine voice.

"Sure."

"I hate to be the one to tell you this," she says reluctantly.

"What is it?" I say numbly, ready to bear whatever bad news she brings. Just when I thought today would be half relaxing.

"Well, um…you see, you need to clean your room," she states, looking disdainfully around at my sixteen years of accumulated junk; some thrown in boxes, others hanging out of suitcases and laundry piles.

"Huh?" I close my journal and smile, relieved at her words. Thank goodness, it's actually not that bad.

"No, I mean, you need to clean your room because…someone's coming to look at the cottage tomorrow."

"Oh," I mutter. So that was what she was afraid to tell me. Well, rightly so. I'm ready to turn hostile to whoever thinks they can walk up and steal my precious childhood home. Of all the nerve!

"That's why Mom and Dad are buying a new stove in a hurry," Kelly mutters, but I barely hear her. My mind is dreaming up ways to steer buyers away from our house.

"We need to sabotage it," I say evenly, peering through the blinds.

Kelly laughs and shakes her head. "Sorry, girl. I know you're really attached to this place."

"And you're not?" I jerk from the window and look her in the eyes.

"Oh, I am. I've cried a time or two about moving. But, you see, I'm ready for change. It's time to move on," she says like a mature adult.

"I'm serious." I ignore her wise words. "We need to make this place unsellable."

"We're fighting a spiritual battle, and we've already chosen to be on God's team. God always wins, remember?" she says with an unapologetic smile. I know she's right.

As I go to bed tonight, I stare up at the green fire alarm dot on the ceiling and tug my blue comforter up to my chest. I've decided to list everything that's shocked me in the past five months aloud since I have my own room, and no one can hear me but God, Charlie, and the green dot.

"First of all, who has a vision that comes true?" I whisper incredulously. "Well, I had one this summer, and then weeks later, I found out I am moving to Oklahoma. But get this—someone is trying to buy our house! They might as well be stealing it. Oh, and I start "real" school in less than a month—just like my vision! Wildest of all, I am trusting a God I can't even see with my entire future. Doesn't that last one sound crazy?" I whisper to the green dot.

But you can see Him! The thought hits me. *You can see who God is and what He does. Think about the prophecies. The vision at camp. Even your own feelings of something happening that is greater than you!*

But I don't want things to change. I argue back. *Things aren't supposed to change!* And I now realize the significance of the inward battle: the battle of the mind. My thoughts are literally determining my actions. Everything I've thought up to this point in life has translated into who Candice is. And I don't want this whole moving-to-Oklahoma drama to ruin my emotional stability. I am determined to process this logically.

You're going to Oklahoma, okay? I tell myself. *No matter what you feel or think, you're going to follow God's will. And I promise there will be blessing, Candice. Just trust Him.*

Trust. Just *trust* Him. If only it were as easy as it sounds. Moving makes all changes in the past seem childish and normal, like the changing of seasons. I keep thinking I'll wake up and laugh about this—like it's some dream I'm imagining. But it's real.

Still, I am moving to Oklahoma whether I feel like it or not, and I must embrace it and move forward. I am learning to be excited to go, even though He's telling me to leave everything I've ever known—my family, childhood home, all of my friends, my school, even my pet bunny Leonardo buried in the backyard—to go to this scary private school.

What's so special about OEH, anyway? I can't answer that now, so I guess I should just be praying I can survive those first few days of being a sophomore. I hope I can make at least two good friends… preferably more, now that I think about it. It's always a good plan to have backup just in case the two friends decide to ditch you. But friends or no friends, I will attend OEH wholeheartedly. After all, I was a trendsetter at my old school. I have a good amount of confidence that I can turn this new private school upside down. Why not?

"I will miss you, little friend," I whisper to the little green dot, who has always been my friend, even when I changed rooms. It hangs in all of the bedrooms in the same corner—right by the door. (I think the same green dot follows me from room to room.)

The green dot blinks back at me without an answer.

"It's hard following God's will. Don't you understand?" I wrestle aloud. *"I…can't…just…leave…"* And before the little green dot has time to answer, my eyelids droop, and I sink into a deep sleep.

"Carissa's Shadow, Part 1"

"Scotty! Come to the hospital!" I hear Mom's helpless voice through Dad's phone.

Dad and I are in charge of driving the first U-Haul of furniture to the rental house. Charlie is sitting in my lap, and I can barely sit normally up here in this crowded compartment. We aren't an hour into the trip when I hear that my little brother Jordan, who was with the rest of the family driving in Mom's car, is in an ambulance headed toward the nearest hospital.

"He's passed out and unresponsive," Dad tells me, pushing the gas pedal. *Well, this wakes me up from my melancholy state of self-pity...*

"Mom said the doctors are saying they can't figure out what's wrong. Everything stops until we figure this out," he adds.

If this isn't spiritual warfare against our family obeying God, what is?

"Jordan is still unresponsive," Mom says hours later on the phone. "Scotty, I don't know what to do...I don't know what to do!" she cries.

"Everything's going to be okay," Dad says, as calm as ever. "God's got this all under control."

"How do you always know?" I whisper to him. Before he can answer, Mom speaks up on the phone.

"The doctors don't know what's w-wrong," her voice quivers. "They said it could be a food allergy or something to do with a brain tumor, or—" Her voice brakes. Dad leans back his head on the U-Haul velvet seat, his eyes on the ceiling.

"Case, we've done all we can do." He draws a deep breath.

"We're praying, Mom," I assure her. And then, more sincerely, I add, "I am praying."

God, forget all my prayers about finding friends at OEH or something happening that will prevent us from moving. Just please heal my brother.

This marks the sixth hour of sitting in this random hospital parking lot in the U-Haul. "May I?" I reach for Dad's greasy box of French fries and try to eat it before Charlie does. After the first hour, Charlie needed to go to the bathroom and eat his puppy chow, so I had to dig in the back of the moving truck for his food and water bowl. Then, I poured a water bottle into his bowl for him to drink. But the air was—and still is—so cold outside that the water quickly froze, so I had to dump out the ice cube and pour him some more.

My mind shifts in between earnest prayers for Jordan's life to how much I hate that this trip happens to fall in the two weeks leading up to Christmas. It feels like the holiday spirit has been cut short. I packed a strand of Christmas lights and blue tinsel to hang in the room Kelly and I will share to remind myself that it's still the holidays. If only I'd known our last normal Missouri Christmas was this past year, I wouldn't have wasted my time whining about not getting what I wanted. At least I'm not *that* selfish anymore.

Still, I'm cold, I'm tired, and I'm itchy in my puffy winter coat. I would have taken it off and turned it into a pillow, but in order to save gas, we've turned off the U-Haul, and it feels like a freezer in here. But I am trying to focus on Jordan. *What if Jordan doesn't wake up?*

"Dad, you mentioned spiritual warfare earlier. Is that like opposition from Satan against God?"

"Yes," he says calmly. "Ephesians 6 tells us we are not fighting against flesh and blood—against things we can see—but by the rulers of the unseen world. People who obey God have targets on them—we are setting ourselves up for opposition from the enemy. So, we need to expect setbacks in life—especially when we choose to follow God's will, like moving to Oklahoma."

"Goodness." I shudder. "So, by moving, I'm literally setting myself up to be attacked?"

Dad laughs. "Just by being a follower of Jesus, you have a target on your back. But God is greater than anything you will ever face. There is no need to be afraid of *anything*. Always remember that."

"Is that why you're not anxious about Jordan?"

"That's right. It doesn't mean I am never scared; it just means I trust in God."

"Easier said than done," I mutter.

"He's awake!" Dad smiles at Mom's texts.

"Thank you, God!" I breathe a sigh of relief. Dad explains that Jordan has blood sugar issues and is hyper-glycemic. Basically, he needed more sugar or something like that. Well, I find that odd…the kid already eats too much candy.

"Mom said he's crying and irritable, but he is going to be okay. You can be glad you're not in *that* car for the next four hours." Dad says, cranking the engine.

"Yeah, that's true," I say. As Dad turns on the heat, the sun is already down. It's a still, quiet night in the hospital parking lot. I think everything is going to be okay. Charlie is asleep in my lap, and we nearly pull off when I remember I left his food and water bowl outside by the curb.

"Wait!" I screech, throwing open the high door to the van.

"Welcome home," the rental house seems to say creepily. It's pitch-black outside, but from my phone flashlight, I can tell the house is dressed in red bricks and gray siding, with a lonely twig tree on the front lawn. The grass is crunchy and dry. Dead leaves blow across the steep driveway. I note the looming clouds overhead. Inside the windows is a hauntingly bare living room, and I can almost hear it saying, *"Come on in, kids,"* in a scary voice. Honestly, the house is probably perfectly fine and normal, but I'm just being overdramatic, as usual… It's almost more fun that way.

"Home sweet home," I joke, hopping out of the truck and letting Charlie sniff the lot.

Juggling his leash in one hand, I push open the door with my foot and immediately feel a rush of cold air. My new home feels like a gray, bleak prison cell. Only this one isn't pretend; I'm going to have to survive here for at least five months. Thank goodness I'll be at school half of the time.

After unloading enough belongings to make it through tonight, I decide to take a nice hot shower.

Only I can't.

"Dad! There's no hot water!" I yell, with shampoo still in my hair. I can't believe this! Where are we, a third-world country?

I probably should've waited to get in until it got warm, but everyone's fighting for a shower, and when you're in a family of eight, you've got to go for it while you can.

I barely survive through the ice water shower and shiver my way into the living room, which is now the complete opposite of bare. There are mattresses, lamps, tall boxes with closet racks, trash bags full of stuffed animals, even a box marked "Charlie" full of his little dog sweaters.

I turn on as many lights as I can in order to make the place cheerier, but then all of a sudden, everything goes black.

"Jordan, stop playing games. Turn on the lights!" I yell in the dark. And then I hear a man's gruff voice on a phone speaker.

"No electricity?!" I mouth in disbelief as Dad walks out of the master bedroom on his phone. I can hear the guy on the other end of the phone saying our house does not and will not have heat or hot water until they can "send somebody up there to fix it."

Maybe I'm seeing things…but I'm pretty sure a little white fur ball just scampered down the hall.

"There's a random dog in the house!" Angel yells. My motherly reflexes lunge at Charlie, who nearly trips out the door and into the unknown. That was a close one.

"Get the dog!" Mom yells, and in desperation, I throw Charlie in a closet and join the family race of who can find the random dog, who is soiling every corner of the white floorboards. *Welcome home, Gibbons family. Welcome home.*

Thankfully, Bria eventually catches the dog, and we find out that it belongs to our next-door neighbors, the Groves.

"I'm so sorry this happened, Chi-Chi's known to do this at night in all of the neighbors' lawns, but he's never done this in anyone's home before," Mrs. Groves apologizes, trying to hold little Chi-Chi in her arms. Malicious Chi-Chi is far more aggressive than Charlie—she's literally biting at Mrs. Groves arms.

"Welcome to the neighborhood!" she adds, but I'm too distracted by Chi-Chi's bite marks on her arms. Apparently, it doesn't faze her.

"We are moving here from Missouri," Mom says. "Our two oldest daughters, Candice and Kelly, are starting OEH."

"Oh, my daughter Lauren is a freshman cheerleader at OEH, and I'm sure she would love to meet your girls," she smiles with a patronizing tone. *Oh, great.* A forced friend who's a freshman cheerleader. Kelly, on the other hand, seems more than thrilled. Thank goodness this isn't the move just yet, or else I would feel as if I were trapped in this gray house with Chi-Chi and Lauren.

I'm supposed to be singing "Jingle Bells" and drinking hot chocolate with Diana in Missouri. I shouldn't be here in this terrible rental house, freezing cold and chasing around a random dog. I should be curled up by our old fireplace watching *The Polar Express*. Seriously, since God has brought us to Oklahoma, can't He provide for our basic needs like heat and electricity?

I spent the night in the freezer (not the actual freezer, though it may have been warmer than my room) and prayed that frostbite wouldn't settle in before my shadow day. Oh, and lo-and-behold, Kelly and I are back to sharing a room. It was fun having my own room while it lasted...

Angel runs into our room with puppy eyes. "I don't want you to go to a real school!"

"I don't want to leave you, Bria, Allison, Jordan, or Charlie either!" I give her a hug. I haven't thought much about how this is going to affect the family. But the more I think about it, Mom and Dad are right; school is going to be the perfect distraction for Kelly and me.

Throughout the next freezing night, I toss and turn over a restless nightmare about OEH. In the dream, I am wearing my trusty pair of overalls, and I'm lost in the endless halls of checkered tiles. Next, I'm standing on a stage with a spotlight on me, forced to give a presentation in front of hundreds of kids, and when I start to speak, everyone laughs at me because of my southern accent.

It's finally morning, and my eyes burn like crazy from lack of sleep. *Absolutely not going to wear those today.* I shake off feelings of dread when I see my overalls hanging crookedly in the closet. I quickly dress in fitted blue jeans and a black athletic shirt, complete with my good old black tennis shoes, thinking no one can critique an outfit as dull as this. I complete my outfit by straightening my hair and applying a decent amount of makeup.

"Who's nervous?" Mom asks in the car. The air is foggy and cold, and it smells like the Christmas season is near. I suck on a mint and reapply a layer of lipstick.

"I'm not," I convince myself, rolling my shoulders to help the ache in my back from sleeping on my makeshift bed.

"I am!" Kelly admits from the front seat, wearing a light gray blouse with her silky blond hair parted evenly down her back.

"Hey, look over there, a Starbucks! We can get coffee there before school on some days!"

"Sure, we can!" Mom supports, merging on the highway. "Candice, make sure to stand up straight when you walk in," she reminds me. This usually bothers me, but this time, I nod and promise to have good posture—because you only have one first impression as a new kid.

Oklahoma Excellence is conveniently seven minutes away, and the drive is all highway. As we turn into the school, butterflies flood my stomach. It is 7:30 a.m., and school doesn't start until 7:45 a.m., but Mrs. Gray instructed us to arrive early at the main entrance, where we will meet our student guides.

The front of the building looks like a typical modern high school, protectively locked until opened by a student ID. *How fancy.*

Kelly rings the buzzer at the door. I shiver in the cold.

"Welcome to Oklahoma Excellence," a lady of medium build and gray, curly hair says as she pushes open the door and welcomes us into the atrium. The ceiling is high and makes her heels, along with our voices, echo like a cathedral. I never thought this would become a reality.

Remember, Candice. If you don't like it, you don't have to go, I comfort myself.

No. I need to pretend I'm stuck here forever. I'll pretend I'm going to a boarding school or something, says logical Candice.

A skylight diffuses sunshine over a fountain and some orchids. The overhead banner reads: "OEH," and I feel as though I might as well be signing up for a life prison sentence.

"Good morning, girls," a woman in a kind voice calls from the office. She is slim, with good posture, wearing a jade green dress, her hair in a tight bun. I automatically stand, assuming she is someone of importance.

"Principal Vanderbilt," she introduces. "Are you the girls who moved here from Missouri?"

"Yes, ma'am," we say in unison.

"Today, you will shadow freshman Eliza Sullivan and sophomore Carissa Carlyle..." She shifts the clipboard in her arm and extends her hand. *Carissa Carlyle.* I replay the name in my head. The name sounds like a girl from a chick flick.

"Psst," Kelly nudges me as a girl enters the office. Cued like a movie, I hear the door swing open from the echoey foyer. There she is.

Her hair is perfectly straight and blond, falling all the way to her waist. Her face is polished flawlessly with makeup. On her neck lies a pink, sparkly stone necklace. She is wearing a white blouse with a blue cardigan and skinny jeans. My heart beats faster with every step as Carissa, placing one foot directly in front of the next, her shoulders turning slightly in stride, reaches the receptionist's desk.

"Excuse me, Mrs. Gray," she asks the receptionist, ignoring the fact that I am obviously a new student sitting nervously on the bench. "Am I supposed to host a student today?"

"Good morning, Carissa. Your shadow student is on the bench." Mrs. Gray gestures toward me. Carissa smirks and pushes her long hair behind her ear, revealing two diamond piercings. I don't realize how short Carissa is until I stand up.

"This is Carissa Carlyle. You will follow her around and get to know OEH," Mrs. Gray instructs, turning to Carissa, who flashes a smile.

"Nice to meet you," she extends her hand as if we are business partners. Her eyes are bright blue and enticing.

"My name is Candice Gibbons; nice to meet you too!" I return the handshake.

"I have to go to my locker before class, so we better hurry," she snaps, then smiles innocently.

"Oh, okay. Have a good day, Kel!" I smile helplessly in her direction.

"Bye, bye!" Carissa waves in a patronizing tone. The atrium is filling with students, and Carissa leads me down a concrete staircase, away from the noise. Her hair smells like tropical shampoo. Her

shoes are black with monogrammed gold letters and look like they're made from genuine leather.

"So, you just moved here from Missouri?" she asks cordially.

"Well, not yet. We're spending our last Christmas in Missouri before officially moving," I reply. It feels so awkward talking about Missouri like a distant memory, especially because I still live there.

"What does your Dad do?"

"He's a pastor," I answer warily, not knowing what she expected.

"Interesting." Carissa raises her perfectly shaped eyebrows.

At the bottom of the stairs, I hear high-pitched voices and the slamming of metal. The halls are lined with bright red lockers, and students dressed in the latest preppy styles. A few stereotypical awkward kids slouch against their lockers, faces glued to their phones, but even they wear name-brand clothes and backpacks.

A group of guys with OEH varsity jackets says something crude in the direction of a few flirty girls near the vending machines. One girl walks over; another just poses. Carissa stops and hugs three of the varsity jackets, and then two girls dressed identically to her.

"Rissa!" yells someone up ahead. The crowd parts to reveal hot red pumps, a boutique jean jacket, and a necklace matching Carissa's.

"This is my best friend, Callie," Carissa explains while Callie parades towards us.

"You forgot to send me the cheer update!" Callie whines in a high pitch. She has deep green eyes, and her face is distinctly defined by her jawbone, and when she smiles, I see her teeth are piercing white. "Who's this?" she whispers to Carissa.

"This is my shadow," Carissa introduces. Callie looks me up and down, from my black tennis shoes to my dad's oversized long-sleeved shirt.

"I am Callie Winters," she finally says, fluttering her fake eyelashes.

"Hello," I say awkwardly. I am completely unfamiliar with this atmosphere. I can't spot a single girl who looks like me.

Two boys swagger over to where we are standing. "Hey!" grunts the first boy with fiery red hair and a mischievous smile. He hugs Carissa.

"Who is this?" says the other boy, who strikes me like a rhino, with metallic spiky hair and a pudgy nose. They've got to be rich. I wonder how such peculiar boys won places with Carissa and Callie.

"My shadow for the day," Carissa laments again.

"My name is Candice Gibbons," I introduce myself, growing more annoyed by the second. Rhino boy extends his hand.

"Stevie Bowers...the third." He bows formally. "I think you look more like a Cassidy than a Candice," he adds awkwardly.

"Oh, for crying out loud," the redhead groans, letting go of Carissa.

"I'm Brett Cline," he shakes my hand. "Stevie's the epitome of awkward," he apologizes. I laugh to ease my own tension. I am desperate to escape Carissa's circle of rich friends. That's when I notice two athletic-looking girls enter the hallway.

They are tall with brown hair—the first two people who remotely look like me. I watch them walk in wearing matching sweatsuits, muscles outlined. Each girl's name is stitched in white on her Nike backpack. As they march past, they acknowledge the other students with a head nod. What confidence.

Carissa taps her watch. "Gotta get my books," she waves and walks away from Callie, Stevie, and Brett. And that's when I put two and two together: every kid is wearing an expensive watch and carrying the latest phone. As in...the latest model. I lapse into abstract social comparison. How can I meet these standards? Apart from noticing everyone's designer clothes, accessories, hair, and nails, I quickly gather that Carissa and Brett are in a relationship. And eventually, I know someone is going to ask me about my relational status.

"Bye, Cassidy!" Stevie salutes in my direction.

I watch Carissa open her locker. It's adorned with glittery cheer pictures, glued atop black and white laminate wallpaper. A pendant light shines over the makeup mirror.

"When you get your locker, you can leave your books in it overnight because most of the homework is online...well, unless you have *Groath*," she warns in a whisper.

"Who's that?"

"You see that classroom with the window covered by the giant poster of a math equation?" she asks. I turn around to see a mysterious door at the end of the hall. It has the word GROATH spelled in big, black letters above the entry.

"That's the freshman math teacher. He's ruthless with homework and makes students carry around big heavy books," she warns with exaggeration in her voice. "But you shouldn't worry about him. Only freshmen kids who are behind go there." She rolls her eyes.

Math, of all the classes! It is my absolute worst subject. I swallow a giant gulp and imagine a camera zooming in on my face. There's no way around this elephant: I am going be a Groath student.

I am snapped out of worry when I see the two athletic-looking girls slam their red lockers and stomp towards Carissa.

"Did you hear what Vanderbilt said?" the taller one questions in a deep voice. Her eyes dart around the room to see if any teachers are listening. Carissa slams her locker and turns her back to me to face them.

"About dress code? Sadly, yes. But being head cheerleader and all, I'm sure I can convince her to change." I am quite certain she threw in that last part about being head cheerleader just for my own knowledge.

"Vanderbilt is a—" Carissa starts to say.

"Shh," the other girl cautions, who is about my height. She nods in my direction to remind them I am listening.

"Who's that?" the taller girl asks, bowing up like she's about to fight me.

"My shad—" Carissa starts to say.

"My name is Candice," I interrupt, clearing my throat. Carissa steps aside, irritated.

"I'm Morgan," says the taller one, whom I'm guessing is close to six feet tall. She reminds me of Diana, but somehow, I can't picture her riding a mule.

Morgan nudges her friend.

"Oh, I'm Afton. Do you play basketball?"

"I was thinking about doing track," I respond offhandedly. As soon as I say those words, I feel a leap in my stomach. I have never done sports leading up to now, so trying out would be a huge risk. And now that I've said it out loud, something tells me Carissa is going to hold me accountable.

"Too bad," says Morgan, looking at Afton.

"Track is great and all; you just have to deal with Stanley," Afton adds, shifting the weight of her sports backpack.

Carissa laughs. "And *that's* why I do cheer. Hey, you could try out to cheer!"

I nearly trip from her words. *Was Carissa Carlyle, the captain of the cheer team, seriously inviting me to join cheer?* I open my mouth to speak, but nothing comes out.

Ahh! A noise startles me.

"Thank goodness it's only the warning bell." Afton double checks her watch.

"See you in chem," Carissa waves to Morgan and Afton, who salute back. As students scatter, I follow Carissa down the checkered floor halls and up two flights of stairs.

"Since this is a Christian school, you'll have Bible class. But as long as you take notes, there's not much to it," she says, pushing open the door. Seven rows of desks horizontally line in the classroom. I watch a short, elderly man limp with a cane to the front of the classroom, resembling a rigid professor. The class is filled with rowdy kids, each appearing filthy rich.

That's when I notice a girl with curly black hair staring at me with a suspicious gaze. She stands at the front of the aisle, peering at me like a black panther to its prey. I try not to look rattled. Slowly, she swaggers over to me.

"Who are *you?*" she crosses her arms, emphasizing it like I've committed a crime.

"M-my name is Candice Gibbons."

"Why are you with *her?*" she scowls at Carissa, who is busy talking with another cheerleader.

"I'm shadowing her for the day," I say innocently, not knowing who is on the bad side. This girl definitely harbors anger towards Carissa, whoever she is.

"I'm Isabelle." She extends a hand. "And you know about dress code, right?" she adds in a low voice.

"Not exactly," I answer, not knowing what to say. *Have I already broken a rule by wearing a black shirt and jeans?*

"Take your seats!" the teacher yells, specifically looking at me. Isabelle retreats to the front of the classroom. Carissa forgot all about finding me a desk.

"Miss…ugh…" the teacher stammers, squinting his eyes at me. In response, the entire class turns around and analyzes me. My face burns red.

"And I was like, 'you have to look at her'…" Carissa continues to talk, giggling with another cheerleader.

"Miss Carlyle?" the teacher taps his cane. When the attention shifts to Carissa, I note Isabelle whispering to another awkward girl while looking in my direction. I catch onto a boy in the front of the classroom eating chicken nuggets and a soda—for breakfast. Then, I notice the girl sitting in front of Carissa is painting on a canvas—in Bible class. "Can't you find a seat for your guest?" the teacher asks impatiently.

Carissa mutters an ugly word and smiles, "Of course, Mr. Tanner." She points to a lone desk against the wall. "You can sit over there." She looks at me dryly. I immediately comply, not waiting for second instruction. But then I try to force myself into the wrong side of the desk and nearly fall over (who knew you could only get in on one side?). Thankfully, the teacher starts to talk, and I don't think anyone notices, except for Isabelle. *That has to be wrong.* I squint in dismay at the wall clock. Is it only 7:44 a.m? This is going to be one long day.

"Carissa's Shadow, Part 2"

It feels like a year has passed. And maybe it did. I feel like I'm living in a new world—one that is ruled by cheerleaders and where people are classified by the clothes they are wearing. On the social side of things, Carissa and her cheerleader friends (and their boyfriends) appear to be "the group." Then there are Morgan and Afton, the athletic girls, who act nice yet unpromising as possible friends, all because I don't play basketball. And then there is Isabelle, who seems to have something against Carissa and her friends. Still, what confuses me the most is Carissa asking me to join cheer. Is she serious?

When the bell rings, Isabelle tries to talk to me again, but I move quicker than her, sticking to Carissa like a baby cub and following her downstairs to her locker so she can retrieve her vegan protein bar.

"Have you ever had these?" she asks, holding the paper-thin snack.

"No," I answer. She grabs a smoothie from her designer lunch bag—the bag that all of the popular girls carry—and slams the locker shut.

"They're *the best*," she testifies, taking a small sip of her pink smoothie.

The next two classes begin and end in a blur. I meet student after student, yet none of them click with me. *Maybe if I run track, I'll make friends.* I resolve, watching groups of matching teammates walk together. All in all, OEH seems like one big hospital. The rooms are sterile, organized, and meticulously decorated in colors of black, white, and red. Everything smells like the alcohol wipes nurses use before giving you a shot.

"This is the technology lab." Carissa walks into a particularly dark room filled with screens. In the center of the room, students are reclining on couches and throwing pillows. The teacher at the front of the class is tall, with dark eyes matching her long curls and skin.

"Sit down!" she yells with the voice of an archangel. I jump at the unexpected sound. We sit next to Callie and Stevie.

"That's Mrs. Lajuana," Carissa whispers, looking scared herself. "She's a beast."

"A beast?!" Rhino boy laughs.

"Shhhh!" Carissa slaps him.

Mrs. Lajuana does seem threatening. I avoid eye contact, which leads me to scan the room. A pudgy boy, who presumes I'm staring at him, winks. A freshman girl at the back is handing out gum. One of the boys with an OEH varsity jacket, whom I had seen earlier, is using a head massager on the girl next to him; she has a pillow in front of her face and appears to be sleeping. I notice another boy who has a beard like a grown man picking at his ear. Gross.

"You, in the back," Mrs. Lajuana calls once class is dismissed.

"Me?" I point to myself dumbly.

"Who else? Come up here," she demands, an annoyed look on her face. Her accent is thick and rather difficult to understand.

"Ooohhhh," some boys sneer on their way out the door. Mrs. Lajuana pays no attention.

"You're awfully quiet," she says, shaking my hand. "Does technology not interest you?"

"Oh y-yes ma'am, it does!" I stammer, searching for the right words.

"Liar!" she laughs. "Well, you already know who I am. What's your name?"

"My name is Candice Gibbons. I am moving here in January." I try to smile.

"Have you ever edited video footage?"

"On occasion," I smile. "I do enjoy editing videos that my family makes." *But it's not like I'm a real filmmaker*, I think to myself, hoping she doesn't ask me to pull up one of our family YouTube video links. *The cringe!*

"Consider joining my journalism class period. We could use a girl like you; all of my students have zero passion for editing," she laments, rubbing her forehead. "But the talent is there," she adds, pointing a finger at her head.

Before I have time to respond, Carissa's shadow looms over my head. "Hi, Mrs. Lajuana!" Carissa turns to me with a dead-serious look, "We have to go to World History."

"Think about it," Mrs. Lajuana clasps my hand. For the first time, I see her crack a smile. I start to follow Carissa into the next class when a towering boy with jet black hair steps in front of me. "This is a bad school," he whispers eerily. I stop, but he turns and disappears into the crush of students down the corridor.

"What just happened?" I mutter aloud. What a creep.

I abandon my search for Towering Boy when I hear '60s music from the classroom behind me. *Why am I here?*

"Idaho is NOT a country!" a curious man whom I presume is the teacher yells, throwing a textbook on the floor. His hair is white and curled in tiny ringlets. His nose is slightly bent to the left. Sweat drips from his forehead. He loosens his top collar and laughs in a grandfatherly tone.

"I can't handle deep questions at this point in my life," he flings himself in his spinning chair. The class chuckles. I take the empty desk beside Carissa, this time sitting down on the right side.

The boy and girl to my right model the picture-perfect couple. The girl has a tailored face and dark eyes, curls trailing down her back. Her fingers are double stacked with rings. She wears a fur vest and glittery Converse. The boy, admittedly handsome, is cloaked in a blue OEH varsity jacket and reflective heart sunglasses. He leans one arm against the girl's desk. The girl stares back knowingly. The soundtrack, which has now switched to *Twist and Shout*, fits these two perfectly.

"Archie!" the teacher screams at an astonishing volume. He cuts the '60s music. Carissa jumps in her seat.

"Sorry, Stanley. Callie and I were discussing politics in America," she lies. *Archie?* Why would Carissa answer to that name?

"Da, da, da, da!" Mr. Stanley trumpets, walking toward me. Oh, please, no.

"Archie, is this your shadow?" he turns to Carissa.

"Why, yes, it is," Carissa smirks.

"Hi, Archie's shadow!" Mr. Stanley shakes my hand wildly. He then notes the confused look on my face and whispers quite close to my face, *"Carissa and I are sworn enemies. She's my archenemy, so I call her Archie."*

"Oh, okay…" I stammer.

"I'm Stanley," he moves back to full volume. "But if you're a track runner, I'm *Coach* Stanley." He turns to some skinny track boys who nod fearfully.

"Be very afraid," one of them adds.

Oh, great.

High ceiling windows make beams of light hit the red tables and colorful art supplies. Carissa's art class is a thrilling hour because it is all girls and mixed with some juniors. I notice the girl who was painting in Bible class slide on the desk next to Carissa. The art teacher, who is young herself, focuses her attention on the series she's streaming on her phone.

"You're Mabrey, right?" I ask, sitting across from Carissa. The art girl glances up from her sketchbook penciled with skyscraper outlines. She brushes her short black hair behind her ear with her wrist. "How'd you know?"

"I read your signature on your notebook," I point out.

Mabrey blushes.

"I'm Can—"

"I'm a glutton for punishment!" a girl wails, walking into the art room with a sparkly notebook tucked under her arm. Another girl whom I have yet to meet follows close behind. They *have* to be upperclassmen, acting with such confidence and looking like they're in college. The talkative one is tan and California-looking, and her friend is model-thin with gloriously red, Ariel-like hair.

"What's up," the tan one says to the teacher, but she's too engrossed with her series. Both girls take seats at the table beside Carissa. Without looking too obvious, I try to listen in on their conversation.

"You really are, Emma," I hear the one with beautiful hair say.

"And what about you, Kinsley? You totally ditched him after your date last night!" Emma says, elbowing her.

Kinsley rolls her eyes. "Rissa over here is dating Brett, you know."

Carissa smirks. "I thought it'd be fun to try him out for a while." Everyone laughs at her response, except for Mabrey. Emma throws a pen to Carissa, who catches it one-handedly.

"You're a player, and everyone knows it," Emma says, lowering her voice in a superior tone. Carissa smiles at the comment. I'm getting the impression she isn't exactly Miss Perfect, whatever the teachers might believe.

Mabrey scowls at the girls and shakes her head with disapproval. Her clothes are plain and wrinkly. The dark circles under her eyes imply she's suffered from a lack of sleep…or she's on drugs.

Emma and Kinsley, on the other hand, are lively and confident. I note their designer clothes and dignified posture. Yet, the class conversation quickly shifts to bashing boys, and the bell could not have rung too soon.

This time, Carissa ignores me on her way to her locker, and Callie meets up with her to walk to the cafeteria. I try to keep pace with them as we walk across the school campus to the student activities center, but it's obvious I'm a third wheel. The wind is frigidly cold, and I am regretting not bringing my coat. But my coat has a stain on the back, and I wouldn't be caught dead in it with the cheer girls. I should probably ask for a new coat for Christmas.

Callie chats a hundred miles an hour while Carissa continuously surveys the boys that walk ahead and behind us. As they open the cafeteria doors, a chorus of voices fills the hall. Most of the students look my age or younger, and each table has a distinct type of teenagers sitting together...definitely all cliques.

"Candice!" I hear a small voice yell above the noise. *Who would call out my name?*

"Over here," the voice says again, and I spot Kelly waving from an all-girls freshman table. I momentarily leave the cheerleaders and find refuge in the table of innocent-looking girls.

"This is Eliza Sullivan," Kelly says, introducing me to a petite girl with blond hair.

"Hello," Eliza waves, munching on a veggie wrap.

"Have you had a good day?" Kelly asks, peering behind my back to see the cheerleaders gossiping at a table, obviously talking about us. I have to make an exit from this cute little freshman table if I have any chance of scoring a shot with the cheerleaders.

"It's been, er...*entertaining*." I hurredly flash a smile, trying to look comfortable. "You?"

"It's been amazing! I can't wait to come to OEH!" Kelly hugs me as Carissa approaches us.

"Are you ready to get your food?" she asks me, wearing the cheesy smile she did when we first met. She walks me to the cafeteria line, where a few lower-class students receive their pizza lunches. I am thankful Carissa stands in line with me, though I realize how this must look to the rest of the student body. As I carry my tray over to the cafeteria table, I quickly realize I am the only one with junk food. Everyone has trim-healthy salads, wraps, and smoothies. I look down at my cold, greasy slice of cheese pizza and try not to gag.

"Everyone, this is Candice Gibbons from...ugh..."

"Missouri," I help, wiping my mouth full of pizza.

Callie lights up with a smile. "Oh! You're the new mayor's daughter who's visiting, right?"

"No, my dad's a pastor." I immediately sip a long gulp of water to avoid further questioning. Murmurs trickle across the table filled with cheerleaders and other model girls. Callie's smile quickly fades, and Carissa changes the subject.

"It's so weird being down here," she says, scanning the room.

"I know," Callie drags out in her valley girl voice, sipping a pink smoothie.

"Do you not eat here?" I ask, confused.

"Are you kidding? Of course not!" says a voice behind me, and Morgan and Afton squeeze in at the table. Now I'm squished beside Callie and questioning everything that's wrong with my body.

"Sophomores can go out to lunch with upperclassmen," Morgan adds, opening her designer lunch bag. "There are tons of places to eat around here—Parsley Bowl, Mountain Smoothie, and tons of Starbucks, of course."

So, that's why no upperclassmen are in the cafeteria... A wave of fear sweeps over me. Pretty soon, they'll find out I don't have a car, and then I'll be outcast at a lonely table in the cafeteria or begging for a seat in Carissa's black BMW.

It's hard to concentrate on the rest of their conversations, so I devote myself to learning all I can about Carissa—her body movements, tone of speech, apparel—everything I would need to fit in at OEH. As I contemplate what I will wear for the first day of school, Callie's words interrupt my train of thought.

"Rissa and I have been friends since preschool," she squeezes Carissa. They look like actresses—no—mall mannequins.

"Aw, that's so great!" I say slowly.

A choke rises in my throat. To them, I am a new girl with zero friends. "I have best friends like that in Missouri," the words fall out of my mouth. Surprisingly, it looks as if Carissa is listening.

"We did *everything* together," I continue. "It was like you and Callie. But now, everything's changing." I stare down at my empty plate. An uncomfortable silence settles over the table.

"That must be hard," Carissa says in an insincere, patronizing sort of tone.

"Can't relate." Morgan mutters, rising from the bench.

"Five minutes until geometry." Callie taps her watch. I feel invisible on the walk back to the main school building. Morgan and Afton talk about spring's upcoming basketball uniforms, while Callie and Carissa talk of all things cheer. I search for Kelly, but she must have left early.

When we walk into the math classroom, I see it is a mostly girls classroom filled with lively voices and the smell of food being passed around. An eccentric teacher with beautiful eyes sits at the table of a desk and converses with Isabelle, who scowls at me as I enter the room. *At least I'll be with Groath.* I remember wondering whether it'd be worse to have a mean teacher or be stuck in the preppy class for my worst subject.

As I find a desk in the back (I've been learning to do that on my own), I watch Callie march to the front of the classroom and begin drawing pictures on the board.

"Ugh, is it a bird?" a familiar male voice yells out. I see Brett Cline enter the classroom and wink at Carissa. Students laugh at his comment. *Hopefully, they won't call on me to answer a math question.* I hope, noting all of the confusing math symbols taped to the walls.

And then I notice the girl who *has* to be the ultimate OEH beauty.

The runway model strides into the room with a boy at each side, wearing skin-tight leggings and cheetah-print heels. She's wearing a black leather jacket with gold hoops on her ears. Her platinum hair is in a perfectly round bun with straight wisps framing her face. Her face fashions that of a model, sculpted and airbrushed impeccably. In her hand are a designer wallet and Starbucks tea. She greets her selected peers, who acknowledge her as Claire Dean, as she sits in a middle seat beside Carissa.

As the teacher takes charge, forcing Callie to erase her animal drawings, I feel more and more like a background character in a teenage reality show. Part of me loves this. I mean, isn't this what I saw in the movies? Everyone seems so perfect here...and there's no way I'd fit in! But then I remind myself I am only being introduced to a certain side of the school. *When I come in January, I'll be able to pick my own friends.* I decide, leaning back in my desk with resolve.

At the end of the day, Carissa happily walks me back to the office.

"If you have any questions when you start in January, just let me know," she hastily pushes open the office door.

"Thanks for letting me shadow you, Carissa," I say with a smile.

"Of course! Oh, and—" she pauses. "It would be fun if you tried out for cheer; tryouts are the first of February," she mentions, hesitancy in her voice.

"Really?" I blurt out in shock. *So, she did mean it!* I can't believe Carissa Carlyle is offering a homely Missouri girl a spot on the OEH cheer squad...not like I want to join, but I am grateful she considers me worthy to ask. "Thanks, I'd love to!" I say against all instincts.

"It's like the best thing ever." She grins, walking out the door.

"Well, we're dying to know how it went!" Mom and Dad ask with excitement over dinner. Everyone is sitting on the ground in a circle (we didn't bring our kitchen table yet), eating pizza (my second time today), and waiting to hear all about OEH.

What am I supposed to say? Faces flash in my mind, from beauties like Claire to threats like Isabelle, from boys like Stevie to the Towering Boy who told me not to come to OEH to even teachers like Mrs. Lajuana who might well invest in my future. *Were the cheerleaders going to be my new friend group? What about track? Stanley? Groath?*

Then God reminds me of the vision I had at camp: being a light to the school. *God, how can I be a light to preppy cheerleaders who look like they've got it all together?* I ask Him.

I guess I'll have to wait until January to see what happens.

"One Last Time"

Childhood is indeed bittersweet. It's as if you view it through rose-colored glasses. And now that we've arrived back home from a trip for the last time, I tell myself to breathe in Missouri's winter richness while the clock is still ticking. No matter how picturesque Missouri summers look, I believe the holidays are even more magical, and I am determined to soak in its beauty. Whether it's the historic white gazebo adorned in Christmas lights, the sound of the church tower bells playing carols by the hour, or the hot chocolate stand brewing in the town square, Ozark is full of holiday spirits.

Memories play in my mind one by one, like during the Ozark Christmas Parade when my former dance team rode in an old-fashioned pickup truck, waving to the townsfolk. I can't believe this is the last time we will drive through the park of sparkling Christmas lights at the Finley River Park while singing classics like *There's No Place Like Home for the Holidays* in our Christmas pajamas.

It's also my last time to hear *The Polar Express* train whistle and toot as it circled around Annie and Papa's Christmas tree, the last time to watch for Poppy through the window dressed up as Santa Claus on Christmas Eve, and the last time to hang the eight gold-stitched stockings on the fireplace mantle and walk down the yellow wall hallway on Christmas morning. Thankfully, there's one last Missouri Christmas to enjoy.

The evergreen trees in our yard covered in a light layer of snow, and red cardinals sit atop the branches. Mr. Coggins' cows have moved to another pasture, so I was able to hop the fence and run in the field by myself this morning. Today the air is thin and crisp, accentuating the smell of evergreen trees surrounding the exterior walls of our house. On the other side of the walls, our little cottage smells of bacon frying and homemade blueberry pancakes drenched in Farmer's Market maple syrup. Children run about dangling Christmas lights and tinsel from their arms. A crackling fire lights up the living room as I spread holiday cheer.

"Deck the halls, everyone!" I yell through the house, throwing wrapped peppermints in the air. "Cheery up, good mates. 'Tis the holiday season!"

"I thought you were depressed about moving," Mom says, confused, passing me in the hall carrying cardboard boxes.

"'Twas true, *mother-o-dear*. But 'tis the last holiday season in the old cottage, is it not?" I pat her on the head. She walks off, shaking her head, not buying my Irish accent.

Don't get me wrong; this holiday season *won't* be the same with everyone's minds on moving to Oklahoma. Next week we are leaving to deliver the first round of moving boxes to the rental house, and I'm beginning to understand why the holidays are so depressing to some people. Like me, people are angry, hurt, or sad, and the music, lights, and holiday cheer don't exactly match up with our feelings. I have new compassion for those who are grieving and just don't feel like celebrating Christmas. But for the sake of ending on a strong note in Missouri, I have decided to temporarily say goodbye to grief and hello to the holiday spirit.

I've been wearing my blue Santa hat with a sparkly "C" on the front every day now, trying to remind myself that it's my decision on how I react to change. Since Mom doesn't feel the need to decorate for Christmas this year, I've taken matters into my own hands and singlehandedly decorated the kitchen. I also directed the rest of the ornamentation as the girls brought down heaps of holiday décor from the attic, even though we only have three days until Christmas because you can't just cut out Christmas, especially in the year my childhood is ending. I even rode with Dad and Poppy in his truck to pick out a Christmas tree at our local tree farm. I mean, since Mom's too emotional to keep the memories alive, somebody has to do it. I will say Mom has been extremely supportive when it comes to having friends over and hosting parties and sleepovers. I know she's trying really hard to make this chapter close on happy terms. But inwardly, something inside of Mom is very dark.

"You seem like a totally different person!" Sophia tells me when she picks me up to go to the Christmas celebration at Silver Dollar City.

"I'm just back to my old, carefree self," I reassure her with a smile. "See? My face is mostly back to normal." I squish my cheeks to show the swelling has finally deflated.

Sophia laughs. "It took you a minute."

"More like six months to get over grieving..." I laugh. "Don't worry, Sophia. I've decided not to cry until we move. I'm going to enjoy my last Christmas no matter what!"

"Your *last* Christmas?" she repeats, merging on the highway.

"My last Christmas in *Missouri*." I playfully punch her arm.

"Good. You had me scared for a minute there," she says with all seriousness, not acknowledging my joke. We are silent for a while, and I decide to turn on the local holiday station to listen to the classic carols. I think we're both realizing it's our last time to see each other for who knows how long, and it's making us unusually solemn.

The wind is so strong it pushes against the car and howls in the cracks of the windows. On both sides of the sloping highway, the Branson hills of trees that used to be filled with red, orange, and yellow colors have turned into brown, bare trees. And though I hate to admit it, the time is feeling more and more ripe to leave Missouri, especially now that I have a glimpse into my life at OEH.

When we pull up to the park entrance, Sophia breaks the silence. "I hope we stay friends after you move."

"Like that's a question!" I retort. "Of course we will; we've been friends since we were three. I am not going to let some silly move come between us."

Sophia smiles with a sincere look in her eyes. "We are growing up, though. Life moves on. I'm graduating next year…"

"Who cares!" I brush off. "Tonight, we are two Missouri friends without a care in the world. Come on, let's enjoy the lights at the park," I say while we get out of the car. "One last time."

Our night is both memorable and exhilarating. For a split second on one of the rollercoasters, while we screamed our hearts out, I was in a state of total bliss. It was one final friendship moment I will never forget.

When we pull up in front of the sad, empty-looking cottage I used to call home, Sophia jumps out of the driver's seat.

"Wait…" she calls, a tiny package tucked under her arm. "Call me sentimental, but I have something for you."

I tug my jacket tighter around my neck and shiver from the cold. "Y-you d-didn't have to do that," I shudder.

"Here," she opens the box for me. Inside is a delicate bracelet chain with a silver charm dangling in the middle.

"See? I have one too." She rolls down her sleeve and reveals a bracelet identical to the one in the box. "Every time we see each other, we'll add another charm. Just like in the movies," she adds, knowing how much I relate movies to life.

"Soph, this is beautiful!" I gasp, holding the chain up to the porch light. And then I place the chain back in its box and give Sophia a hug. "Don't forget to trust God even when things don't make sense."

"Like you're doing," she says, her words muffled in my coat.

"Yeah. It's hard, but we have to stay strong in God. Cause who else will we trust?"

"Yeah."

"And Sophia," I release from the hug, "you're a senior, which practically has the word 'leader' attached, so keep inspiring others," I tell her.

"You too, world changer." She punches me in the arm. "Your name means 'Full of Light,' so go turn that school upside down."

"I will, Soph. I will," I promise.

"Hand me two red gumdrops, will you?" Catherine asks me, holding out her hand. "I need them for my fireplace."

"Here." I reach into the gumdrop bowl and throw them across the counter.

My Christmas season is never complete without the Brick's annual Gingerbread House Contest at Lexi's house. Since this is my last time to attend, I am determined to create my best Gingerbread house yet. Everyone is fervently competing for one of the three categories for the best house: creativity, originality, and best overall display.

Diana is sitting beside me. We are both aware this is our last time to see each other before I move. Oklahoma seems so far away from this table of security…

"It's not like you're moving far away," she says out of nowhere, as if she could read my thoughts. "I mean, what's the drive like from here to OKC?"

"About five hours," I acknowledge. "But it still seems like another country."

"You need to get your license," she tells me with a smirk, pushing me to face my fears. "Then you can drive back whenever you want."

"True," I laugh. "But getting my license is the least of my worries right now."

"Candy Cane?"

"Huh?"

"Can you pass the candy canes?" she asks.

"Oh, sure."

"But think about it. You have your license; it's an automatic fit-in with the girls at school, right?" Ella adds, overhearing our conversation.

"I guess. But my parents want me to earn a car, remember?"

"Oh, yeah. Scratch that," she sighs.

"Well, I'm sure you'll still make friends," Catherine says cheerfully at the end of the table, remembering what it was like when she moved to Missouri. "Y'all were so friendly to me when I moved here; I'm sure you'll get the same in return."

"Thanks, Cat!" Kelly and I say in unison. It happens all of the time.

"Your two-story Gingerbread house is coming along great!" Lexi praises right when one of my little gummy bear characters living on the second floor falls over. "Keep it up!" she gives a thumbs up.

"Somebody ought to make Harvey the bunny live in their Gingerbread house," Grace says with a smirk.

"Harvey! Harvey! Harvey!" Everyone chants again. I'm going to miss all of our inside jokes.

As we wash our hands and prepare for the judging of our houses, Diana pulls me aside with an envelope in her hand.

"I want to send you off to Oklahoma with this letter in my hand. You're not allowed to read it until you are on the road."

"I won't," I promise, giving her a hug. *"Goodbye, Diana."* She returns the hug with a gripping squeeze, reminding me of her loyalty, honesty, and unwavering friendship.

"We'll see each other again." She winks. For whatever reason, I believe it with all my heart.

"And the winner of the best overall Gingerbread house of this year's annual contest goes to...*number 11!*" Lexi's mom exclaims.

"Way to go!" Everyone congratulates. I clap and scan the room, but seeing everyone is looking at me, I peak at the number beside my Gingerbread house and realize I was indeed the winner. I couldn't care less about winning a Gingerbread house contest, but I am thankful to end my three years winning streak strong.

"Thank you, thank you," I bow dramatically.

When it's time for Kelly and me to leave, all of the Bricks escort us to the car.

"I'll help!" Ella offers, grabbing some of my sleepover luggage as I juggle my Gingerbread house (half of it has crumbled, but I've decided to keep it because it will still taste delicious).

On the driveway, Mom hugs each of the Bricks, and everyone automatically forms into a circle—just like we always did at the end of a Bible study.

"Well, Bricks, this is it," she says, and by the look on her face, Mom was crying on her drive here. It's the first time I've seen her with evident signs of grief. I know she loves the Bricks just as much as I do.

"You can always drive back for class once a week, you know," Lexi offers kindly.

"I wish," Kelly responds to Lexi. Images of junior high and high school memories with the Bricks play in my head—all of the sleepovers and videos and inside jokes. Carissa and her friends would never understand.

As I hug each of the Bricks and say a few personal words of encouragement to each one, I pray that God will send me new friends with the same characteristics of godliness, loyalty, and genuine hearts. Oh, how rare these qualities are in friends! I wish I could walk in with the Bricks arm in arm on the first day of school. And yet, I realize I must face the cold, sterile school halls, just me and God.

Goodbye, Bricks. I will miss you more than you will ever know.

There's one final person I must see before the year closes: my fellow PK, partner in crime, and "twin" sister, Jaclyn.

I know her schedule is chaotic. I cannot imagine the pressure she faces, and I won't pretend to understand what it feels like to be an honor student, leader of FCA at her school, swimmer, track runner, band member, kids volunteer, and small group leader. Jaclyn has pushed me to be the girl I am today. Whether it's signing up for a mission trip, hosting student podcasts, or simply stepping out of my comfort zone each Wednesday, I am forever grateful for her example. She's taught me to push myself in all areas of life, whether I am naturally good at them or not. She also taught me the heart of being a servant at church.

I am grateful to spend an afternoon at her family's cabin-style home, which houses a quietness I am certain will never enter the house of the Gibbons due to all of the children living under one roof. After feasting on Christmas cookies and reliving memory after memory, we drive to the jewelry store in between our houses to meet up with my mom. The jewelry store happens to be in front of a movie theater, and the music is quite loud. At first, I'm annoyed because it's breaking up our tender moment. But then Jaclyn lifts a finger to her mouth.

"Shhhh…do you hear the song that's playing?"

"Oh, my goodness…" I stop to listen. "It's our song! The melody we listened to during the ten-hour mission trip to Tennessee!"

"That's crazy!" she exclaims.

I can't believe they're playing our song right here at this moment! I feel the need to say something—do something—to show her how appreciative I am of her example, but she beats me to the chase.

"I made something for you," she says, opening the trunk and revealing a neatly wrapped gift bag.

As our song crescendos to the chorus, the December wind seems to stop for a moment while I open the gift. "Jac, no way! You made this?"

"It's a photo collage of a few of our memories over the years. I couldn't fit all of the pictures, so some of them are on the back…" she says, helping me with the tissue paper. The background of the giant picture frame has the cutout of the state of Missouri in the far-left corner, with little connecting dots leading to the state of Oklahoma in the far-right corner.

"I made it, so you won't forget your roots…" she says with a smile, pointing at the heart representing Ozark in the cutout of Missouri.

"I will hang this in my room as soon as I get there!" I say, and then Mom pulls up and is ready to leave.

"Oh, um…I guess it's time to say goodbye," I mumble. Our song is fading off in the distance, as if telling us to say goodbye.

"Just for now," she says humbly. "Goodbye, Candice."

"Goodbye, Jaclyn." I squeeze her neck. "Thank you for…for… *everything.*"

"Goodbye, Childhood"

Six children and a dog walk across the dry winter field hand in hand. The harsh December wind stings our ears, and we tug our coats tighter around our necks. It is silent and dreary: the perfect bleak weather for our last moment at the cottage.

Memories of running through the grass in the springtime flood in my mind, like when we wore sundresses and braids and danced in the grass or flew kites while running around aimlessly until we were caught adrift. I remember how we liked to pretend we could climb trees, but the idea came to a halt the day young Kelly tried to climb a Maple tree and got too scared to climb down, so she spent the entire afternoon in the branches. At least we had high hopes of what we could play outside—in our childhood minds, anything was possible.

More memories come to mind, like the times we would cover ourselves in sidewalk chalk from head to toe or cake mud on our arms to let it bake in the sun, all of them followed by the picture of Mom chasing us with the water hose to give us an outdoor bath. Our favorite thing to do was to stuff a flour tortilla in the pocket of someone's coat and later split it into pieces for our "supper" when we played "house" at our playground called The Mantis. *Oh, our dear playground.*

"We can't even bring it with us," Bria mourns bitterly, glancing over her shoulder at its familiar structure.

"Childhood is over," I lament.

"No, it's not," Kelly retorts, wrapping her arms around Angel, who's shivering with cold. "We are beginning a *new* chapter of our childhood."

"Yeah!" says Allison, carrying little Jordan. "But I will miss being able to run around in an open field."

"Me too," Bria says, reaching for a fallen branch to use as a walking stick. "Well, their childhoods may not be over, but mine is."

We stop to rest at the top of the hill, overlooking miles upon miles of hills and farmland. Sitting in a circle, I pass around a bit of tortilla from my coat pocket and place it in each person's shivering hands. We nibble the bread in silence. It is cold, but that is not what stings the most. It is the deep, nagging feeling inside that childhood really is over. I will never have this moment again.

At the bottom of the hill sits the tiny, yellow cottage, smoke rising from the chimney. Before the furniture was removed, anyone who stepped one foot in our door would instantly know the cottage was adored by six homemakers; that the children inside loved this house with its mix-matched decor, paint-stained walls, and name carvings on bedroom floorboards. I'm sure it will make a wonderful home for another family...

"Kids! It's time to go!" Mom's voice echoes in the distance, ringing the hanging chimes on the porch.

It seems she always calls us at a time when we are at the climax of a marvelous game of make-believe. But today, it's different.

In my mind, I am being called away from childhood.

I seize the hands of those around me. "We may leave our home, friends, and family, but we aren't going to leave each other," I say solemnly. Bria and Allison nod at my statement. Angel is silently crying.

"This is a calling—an adventure..." Kelly adds. "And the Enemy is going to fight for our attention. Remember, we will be facing spiritual warfare. There will be opposition, but we've got to remember why we are going to Oklahoma."

I close my eyes and envision the hallway. My mission is school. I don't know who they are yet—be it Carissa or Mabrey—but I know God has me on a specific assignment at OEH. My mission is people.

Mom rings the chimes once again. They sound like the mourning of the church bell tower in the distance, which happens to be ringing alongside them. Both wail like the cries of our Missouri home, begging us not to leave. *Don't leave! Don't leave! This is your home!*

"Let's run through the field. One last time," I announce. And so, with the breeze at our back, we fly through the field, laughing and screaming down the hill.

For some people, childhood ends slowly, like the changing of seasons. And though mine feels as though it is ending in a sudden instant, I am grateful leaving Missouri has evolved over the past six months and not weeks—or even days—like some people's lives.

I am a mature sixteen now, and perhaps I am evolving into a mature Meg and not so much an immature child. It does not make my grief any easier, but I refuse to be selfish and self-serving, ignoring the call God has on my life. I refuse to settle to be a mediocre Christian. If I am going to follow Jesus, I am going to do it wholeheartedly. I am ready for all that God has for me in Oklahoma.

January 4th

I am snapped out of sleep by the sound of my 7 a.m. alarm. The room is pitch black, and Angel is sleeping soundly on the floor. Mom and the rest of my siblings stayed at Annie and Papa's house overnight, while Angel and I stayed with Gigi and Poppy.

Our little yellow cottage is officially emptied. The lights are off, the rooms are bare, and the doors are locked. We can never go back.

At first, I forget about this, and my sleepy eyes search the room. *Where is Charlie? This bed is much too big to be my own*, I think to myself. The sheets are soft, Egyptian linen, and I am surrounded by a host of pillows. A dull fan hums to the left of the bed, and soon the faint smell of Gigi reaches my nose, a mix of cherry blossoms, vanilla shampoo, and childhood memories. I stretch my legs until my bare toes touch the end of the mattress. *I'll sleep another hour*, I decide, letting out a deep yawn.

Oh, my goodness. I shoot up in bed. *Today is the Big Move.*

My heart is beating like the drums at a pep rally. I leap out of bed and mentally put on my leadership hat so I can help Dad. He is carrying a thousand pounds of stress, and I am going to need to care for Angel and Charlie. Today isn't going to be easy, but it's what I have to do, so I am going to embrace it.

I quickly dress in a blue sweatshirt and jeans in the cold bathroom before tiptoeing down the staircase to the kitchen. Bits of snow remain outside from a blizzard of winter last night. Wind howls down the chimney and blows smoke ashes into the hearth room, situated to the left of the kitchen.

As I walk down the winding grand staircase, I smell the nostalgic scent of Poppy's coffee. I can already tell he has made his famous big breakfast like he's done my entire childhood. I try not to think of it as our last time to eat together, for who knows if I'm never coming back. Still, you never know…

"Morning, Poppy!" I greet giving him a hug.

"I made your favorite," he says, hugging me. Dad quietly enters the kitchen.

"Smells great." Dad's wearing two hoodies because of the chill. We fill our plates and eat in the hearth room. No one mentions the obvious fact that we are about to move. January 4th has been marked on everyone's calendars—mine as the *Big Move*. Well, it *was*. My calendar is packed in one of the thousands of moving boxes at the moment.

I am currently choosing not to live in the present. It's my way of coping, like self-preservation. Angel hazily walks into the room beside Gigi, who's wrapped in her shawl and sniffling quietly. Dad glances at the grandfather clock across the room. He turns to Poppy and nods. Poppy then rises and collects our plates. I flinch when a hand touches my shoulder. It is Gigi, and she's whispering something in my ear. I feel her kiss my cheek and walk out of the room.

Everyone has left. I am sitting by myself in silence.

I've turned the page of my Sundays at Annie and Papa's house, snuggling on the couch and watching our favorite shows. No more Cruising Tuesdays with Annie, singing at the top of our lungs. I will no longer sit beside Gigi and talk about future plans together. No more afternoons in Poppy's Garden. There won't be weekends at barn parties, running on the hidden trail with cousins, or exploring mysteries in the woods. No more porch swing talks with friends. No more freedom in my homeland. Everything's over.

Life has many seasons, and this one is over. I am not going home. We *have* no home. It is time to say goodbye to Missouri, goodbye to childhood. I won't ever lie at the pool beside Sophia and plan summer activities. The days of sitting by Jaclyn at youth or riding the bus with her to camp are over. Diana and I will no longer be schoolmates or ride horses in her field. My relationship with the Bricks is a thing of the past. They will move on without me and travel to Europe and make new memories. My season of childhood bliss has faded away, never to return. Everything's over. Done. Complete.

I can't explain my grief other than it is beyond anything I've ever felt before. *Grief is okay.* I tell myself. Grief reminds me that I'm human. But I must not allow my grief to stand in the place of my faith. In this season, I choose to trust God with everything.

I trust God, even though everything in me fights against it.

I trust God because He's God, and I'm not.

There is something new He has for me. A new adventure in store. What I am about to experience will call for an even greater level of trust.

And so, at the ripe old age of sixteen, I close this chapter of my life in Missouri. Perhaps someday, I will write about all of my childhood memories. But for now, my final chapter in Missouri is finished.

Goodbye, childhood.

The Lord had said to Abram, "Leave your native country, your relatives, and your father's family, and go to the land that I will show you. I will make you into a great nation. I will bless you and make you famous, and you will be a blessing to others."
—Genesis 12:1-2

Acknowledgments

A Time to Trust would forever be swirling around in my head if not for the delightful team at Trilogy Christian Publishing. Specifically, I would like to thank Mark Mingle for seeing potential in my original rough draft and offering me a contract; the WorldMissionMedia/ Trilogy editing team for providing editing expertise; Ariel Soltero and the entire design team at Trilogy for their beautiful design work of *A Time to Trust*; and most of all, Melissa Miller for guiding me along the publishing process through countless emails and inquiries. It was a pleasure working with Trilogy on my first book.

A special message of gratitude goes to Nancy Backues, the first person who read my manuscript. My deepest sympathy for her family as Nancy passed away before the release of this book. She was a beloved friend to our family, gifted writer, and faithful servant to God. You can read her personal and positive journey with cancer in her book *Unshakable* on Amazon.

My highest respect is directed to my parents for wholeheartedly supporting my dream to be a published author: Dad, I can still see the glimmer of amusement in your eyes as you listened patiently to your first-born ramble about chapter titles. You lead me right, and my success points to your wisdom. Mom, thank you for leading the way by writing *A Girl's Life with God* (Arise, 2003) and lifting my spirits as only a fellow writer can achieve. Your kindred spirit provided much-needed comic relief and motherly support in between my drafts, like the way you softly knocked on my door to deliver a *"bit o' bread"* for the *"poor soul."*

I must point out that Kelly Grace, Bria, Allison, Angel, and Jordan are, in fact, the real names of my siblings, though I almost changed Allison's name to Penelope but decided against it, seeing as though Allison might be offended (she later confided in me that she would not). So, Kelly Grace, Bria, *Penelope*, Angel, and Jordan: I am grateful that each of you expressed such grace, understanding, and privacy during writing hours. Though writing a book was not your dream, you adopted it as such. *Ne cures, domum nostrum iterum aliquo die ememus. Tu modo exspecta!*

In an excited squeal, I want to say, *"We did it!"* to my closest companions: Poppy, Gigi, Papa, and Annie. What was once a sentimental stroll along Poppy's Garden or a rock on Annie's porch swing became the foundation on which *A Time to Trust* was built. Without their generous hospitality (and a good supply of green apples), this procrastinator would certainly not have finished a *real* book, let alone enjoyed the process. Quite literally, every chapter was written within their homes. And so, I dedicate this book to them. A special thank you to Papa for capturing the beauty of the Midwest on the front cover photograph of *A Time to Trust.*

Of course, this section would be incomplete without acknowledging my dear Missouri friends who sent me off to Oklahoma with a skip in my step and joy in my heart. Diana, Jaclyn, and Sophia are not real people, but they represent the personalities of my closest friends. To them, I say thank you for expressing straightforward criticism and cheering me on through the dark days of writer's block by offering hot chocolate teas and retelling forgotten details tied to the stories in this book. I value your deep friendships and loyalty.

Lastly, to the Bricks—who *are* a real thing—I miss our lunch table jokes and short story competitions, and I do pray all of you are healthy and full of the joy of the Lord—wherever you are in the world. Until we meet again, I send my warmest regards to our beloved Mrs. Meyers, invisible Harvey, beautiful Amber, and especially contrary Dillon. *Laterem semper laterem!*

Sixteen-year-old Candice is about to enter the world of a private schooler…and it's *not* like the movies.

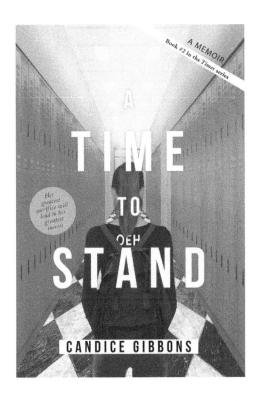

Join Candice in Book #2 of the *Times* series as she discovers the sacrifices that follow obeying God's will. *A Time to Stand* dives into the world of cliques, quirks, and social cues, all while tackling real issues like depression and the temptations of compromise.
Best of all, it's a world based on true people and events.

Coming soon in 2022

About the Author

Candice Gibbons, now a senior in high school, believes you too can have the joy of the Lord amidst adversity. Like now, as she writes from the windy plains of Oklahoma, she continues to enjoy life with her dog, C. S. Lewis, her fish, Chesapeake, her cello, Quincy, and her new cactus, Spikey. Candice surrendered her life to God at age ten, but only until she moved did she fully submit her life to Him. She hopes you are encouraged and inspired to trust God through your difficult situation no matter what. Stay up to date by following her on Instagram @author_candicegibbons or by reading her latest work on her website: candicegibbons.com.

CPSIA information can be obtained
at www.ICGtesting.com
Printed in the USA
LVHW030841200422
716605LV00007B/455

9 781637 692127